THE GREAT TELECOMS SWINDLE

KEITH BRODY • SANCHA DUNSTAN

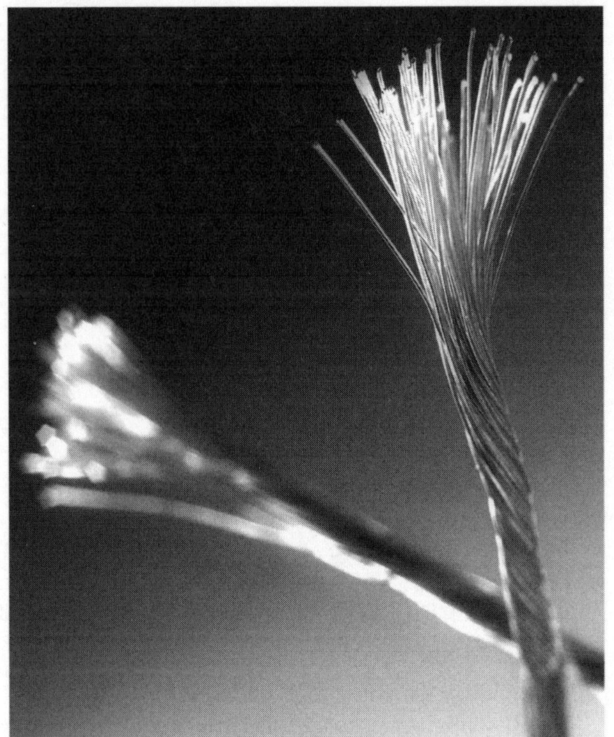

THE GREAT TELECOMS SWINDLE

HOW THE COLLAPSE OF WORLDCOM FINALLY EXPOSED THE TECHNOLOGY MYTH

CAPSTONE

First published 2003 by
Capstone Publishing Ltd (A John Wiley & Sons Co.)
8 Newtec Place
Magdalen Road
Oxford OX4 1RE
United Kingdom
http://www.capstoneideas.com

British Library Cataloguing in Publication Data
A CIP catalogue record for this book is available from the British Library

ISBN 1-84112-467-2

Typeset by
Forewords, 109 Oxford Road, Cowley, Oxford
Printed and bound by
T.J. International Ltd, Padstow, Cornwall

This book is printed on acid-free paper

Contents

Acknowledgements

Our parents, Lawrence and Patricia Brody and John and Sara Dunstan, without whom…

Over the years, many people (all friends and respected colleagues) have made enormous contributions to our work both inside and outside telecoms. This project and many others we have undertaken would have been impossible – as well as far less enjoyable – without them. We express our gratitude in particular to: Chris Wilmott, Julian Bright, Margrit Sessions, Stewart Anderton, David James, Geoff Devlin, and Sheila Von Rimscha.

It takes a team to make a book, and we were lucky to have the best behind us. Capstone–Wiley held our hands, gave orders, cajoled us along, and generally made things happen. In particular, profound thanks to the ever-inspirational Mark Allin, long time colleague, visionary publisher, and ace tennis player (without whom we'd have spent less time on the court and would have thus delivered these pages earlier. On the other, had we done so, this book would have published before anyone at WorldCom had actually entered a guilty plea. That's the silver lining in a 0–6 loss).

Lastly, and especially, profound thanks to Michelle Bryce and Caroline Hughes who have, very simply, made this book possible whether they know it or not. The next generation is safer in their hands, than it is in the hands of many of those who feature in the pages that follow!

Thank you, also, for choosing to read this book.

Preface

This book is written for the general reader. We've "covered" – which is to say written about, investigated, and analysed as journalists, researchers, and consultants at different times – the telecoms market for a number of years. For the most part, we've written for a specialist readership or we've given presentations to "insider" audiences, which is to say those already working in the telecoms industry.

Those "specialists" will have their own views of what lead to the Great Telecoms Swindle, some of which will concur with our own and some of which probably won't, but many of which, either way, have been generously contributed by their holders in the course of writing this book.

Our hope is that in the pages that follow, the general reader will find an interesting, exciting story (albeit a small reward by way of offsetting the money that many will have lost in the telecoms market crash). We have tried, where possible, to avoid the overly technical and if this book is liberally spiced with our own opinions and personal reflections, and in some cases simplifications, that's because we're setting out to write our "ground-up" view of what's gone on in telecoms in recent years for a readership we're assuming has little prior knowledge of the subject matter.

We don't claim that our conclusions are "right" in the exhaustive sense of the word as, after all, we are not presenting an analytical report here. But they represent what we experienced, and what we think to be the case where the fall of the telecoms market is concerned.

We hope this book enlightens, and we hope it's an enjoyable read. We also hope that to some extent it lifts the veil which tends to shroud the corridors of corporate power, and permanently disabuses the general reader (or, for that matter, worker) of the oft-held but seriously misguided notion that those at the top of the industrial food chain are any more competent than the rest of us simply by dint of the fact that "they are there". There is a tendency to think that any industrial or commercial disaster must somehow have its roots in complexity . . . in issues that are somehow beyond the ken of the average person. That is far from the case, as we hope the conclusions in this book make abundantly clear. Idiots rise to the top, too.

In the world of telecoms we met a lot of highly successful corporate leaders who, daily, made million- and even billion-dollar decisions. They wore expensive suits, sat in spectacular offices, were invariably accompanied by a retinue of lackeys trailing behind them; were to all intents and purposes almost "stars" in their own business world. And an awful lot of those people proved to be more or less complete dunces, now hoist by their own petard, when it came to leading their businesses.

The Great Telecoms Swindle is loosely divided into two parts. In the first, we cover the changing nature of the telecoms industry in the 1980s and 1990s. This period, which might be hallmarked by the phrase "all change", was in retrospect the fertile breeding ground for the direct causes of the crash. In the second part of the book, we chart the events of recent months and attempt to put them into some sort of perspective.

Interspersed throughout the book, we shall look at crash-related events at closer quarters by following in more detail the decline and fall of specific companies within the telecoms market. In these "case studies", the tale of the actual crash and, as we see it the Swindle, is revealed in relief.

Literally hundreds of telecoms-related businesses have gone under during the past eighteen months, from all corners of the industry, ranging from service providers to equipment providers to infrastructure providers and others. To choose only a handful of stories from such a menu of available choices requires an arbitrary decision be made. It would be near impossible to come up with a "representative" list, at least without writing an encyclopaedia.

Our choice has been, obviously, to include WorldCom, the company whose fall effectively added the monicker "Swindle" to what was already recognized as a crash, and the start of whose story we relate in the first chapter of this book. Fairly, but possibly even unfairly, WorldCom has come to stand for everything that defines the events now taking place.

We add Lucent Technologies, Global Crossing, NTL, and Marconi to the list. Global Crossing's tale is not entirely dissimiliar to that of WorldCom. The story represents the demise of another major carrier and WorldCom competitor and a demise that came to light marginally in advance of the

WorldCom story revealing itself. There is, frankly, very little more tasteful in the Global Crossing story than in the story of WorldCom itself. It says much that the two companies are now widely known as WorldCon and Global Double Crossing.

The fall of Lucent Technologies, which as we write struggles desperately for life under ever new management (and may yet, against the odds, make it), is at least as spectacular as the fall of any other player in the crash though perhaps marginally less widely reported in some quarters. This is a company that in many respects had it all, and ended up with nothing. Lucent was, and is, a telecoms giant brought to its knees by incompetent management on a scale that almost defies comprehension. Lucent was once the engine room of the entire telecoms industry.

And Marconi, once an old-school manufacturing powerhouse that joined the telecoms boom with a massive cash pile in hand like Lucent squandered a heritage almost unrivalled (within British industry) in barely a matter of months. Lastly, NTL, a microcosm of macrocosms. The triumph of style over substance. Barclay Knapp sold the goods to Wall Street, but his customers apparently never received them.

The pin-up boy of the Great Telecoms Swindle has, by default, become Bernie Ebbers, former CEO of WorldCom, if only because every story needs a peg on which to hang its headlines and scandal conveniently thrust Ebbers into the limelight.

We, however, would have the faces of Lucent's Rich McGinn,

Marconi's George Simpson, and Global Crossing's Gary Winnick affixed to poles outside the doors of our own telecoms hall of shame, at a minimum alongside if not ahead of Ebbers' own. If, ultimately, criminal wrongdoing is proved at WorldCom, then the prospectively indicted executives of that company would in our estimation end up as nothing more than common criminals. The Great Telecoms Swindle was not caused by their ilk; it was, rather, caused by village idiots instead. The lunatics who found themselves in possession of the keys to the asylum.

Lastly, those readers who wish to share their views or reactions to *The Great Telecoms Swindle* with the authors are encouraged to contact us through our publishers.

Enjoy the book!

Keith Brody and Sancha Dunstan
Oxford, October 2002

Introduction

In October 1999, we found ourselves on a plane bound for Geneva, where we were to attend the International Telecommunication Union's (ITU) quadrennial global telecoms summit, a jamboree of Babylonian proportions at which the great and the good of the communications industry gathered in an orgy of self-congratulation.

We were decanted from our EasyJet budget flight (proving that largesse is not always extended to journalists, whatever you may think) in the company of a reporter friend who told us that, as he'd been unable to secure a hotel room within two hours of the city, he'd be commuting back and forth from the Luton Airport TravelLodge for the next four days. Something of an inconvenience, you might think, but no matter. Everyone in the industry had money to spend and no one was going to risk missing out on the big party.

Making our way via a series of labyrinthine underground passages from the airport arrivals hall, we emerged into a summit site of which Mammon himself would have been proud had dark fibre been his line of business. You want impressive telescopic exhibition stands? Here were multi-tiered skyscrapers, more like! Bells and whistles, fountains and mountains, and though we can't quite remember exactly where, in all probability dancing girls, too. No expense had been spared. A series of aircraft hangars stood before us in which the robber barons of the modern communications world had gathered atop their makeshift Acropolis to boast (censored first by their retinue of

PR people), that "mine is bigger than yours." We didn't know then, but we do now, that the "bigger" they were referring to was probably their debt ratios.

In those heady Arcadian days, the telecoms market was awash with money, happiness, and optimism. It seemed like a great place to be. There were no cumulus clouds gathering on the horizon. Only an unbridled sense of future riches as far as the eye could see: new opportunities (for profit) presented themselves like a row of sitting ducks waiting to be exploded. The summit themes might as well have been "devices" (progressive technology) and "desires" (cash).

In the weeks before the ITU event, one of us (Keith) had sat on the judging panel for the Financial Times Global Telecoms Awards, prizes designed to identify and honour industry leaders in various appropriate categories with, it seemed, a much vaunted kudo presented in the name of Britain's prestigious pink sheet. Much coveted? Well, anybody could enter, and it seemed that most everybody did. Some of them even sponsored the gala, too.

The "Oscar for Best Actor", which is to say the top banana award (it being subsequently won by 2 Monkey) in the line up of baubles on offer saw a short list of five names vying for the nomination of telecoms' equivalent to "Man of the Year". We cannot now remember all five, but two of them, including the eventual winner, were Rich McGinn, the then chief executive officer of Lucent Technologies (who, we now know, was in the process of running his company almost into the ground) and Bernie Ebbers, the chief executive officer of MCI Worldcom as it then was (whose company now appears to be on the verge of complete implosion amidst the flurry of accounting scandals which inspired us to write this book). Given the preceding facts, it will not surprise you to learn that Bernie Ebbers won. And no, Keith didn't vote for him. It will do my credibility little good to admit that in the initial ballot, I put my weight (such as it was) behind McGinn. I admit to this now solely for fear that a fellow judge will remember, and expose me.

It is, perhaps, equally unsurprising with the benefit of hindsight to learn that Ebbers' penchant for cowboy boots and his past vocation as a basketball coach were considered as newsworthy at the time as his telecoms knowledge and industry acumen. We live in a celebrity culture, a fact which is reflected in the market position in which the telecoms industry now finds itself.

The business leaders in those glory days between 1998 and 2000, most certainly turned the focus away from the fundamentals underlying their companies, and created a cult of personality instead. The public, with its insatiable appetite for trivial and superficial personal detail, must take some responsibility for allowing this to happen. What a price they have paid for doing so.

When we think of Orange, we think of innovative branding (corporate personality) and the enigmatic Hans Snook (visionary leader). When we think of Vodaphone, we are invariably reminded of its cricket-loving helmsman in the same breath in which the epic Mannesman deal that he engineered is mentioned. Without touching on the size of Chris Gent's annual bonus which, it often appears, is the subject of controversy simply because of its size, rather than because of any relationship it might bear with the numbers on the company's balance sheet.

At times, it seemed like Messrs Bonfield and Vallance, the British Telecoms leadership double act who actually did manage to avoid crippling debt, if without steering BT anywhere in particular, were reviled simply for their shortcomings in the style department (they didn't have any). Still, better to end up unemployed and smiling knowingly than to find yourself taking up a new job sewing mailbags, which is what some of their peers may yet end up doing if the US Congress and President Bush get their way.

It thus says much about our age that investors, small and institutional alike, so haplessly and willingly took their eyes off the ball. Or perhaps this story's other whipping boys, the community of "financial analysts" (we cannot bring ourselves to use the prefixes "independent" or "expert") did it for them. Pages and pages of irresponsible "buy" recommendations which amounted to little more than a public display of mutual masturbation between the financial and telecoms communities gave significant momentum to the industry wave, lubricating the passage through which money disappeared into the communications black hole. Today, the financial community sits discredited. Its members, too, are likely to find themselves in court before too long.

We found, in our work as journalists and consultants, that the soundness of a telecoms company was often reflected in one telling observation: the less noise it made, the better things probably were. Trouble was, so few companies declined the opportunity to draw attention to themselves that it'd have taken a master cynic to grasp that the majority were really in as much trouble as they now appear to be. But time has proved that it was those were claiming to be re-inventing the telecoms wheel on a weekly basis in 1999 that are deepest in trouble today.

In a sense, how such a thing as the telecoms crash could happen, how men who were leading their businesses into the abyss could simultaneously be picking up "Man of the Year" trophies is what this book is about. It's an overview of a roller coaster ride that now dominates the daily news pages and in many ways affects us all. Why did it take so long for the business world to recognize that the emperor was wearing a new set of clothes? As Lear said, "when we are born, we cry that we are come to this great stage of fools".

The answer, of course, is that no one wanted to see, let alone to believe the truth though in many ways the warning signs were there. As a result, miles of fibre was laid, and then the money was raised to lay some more. Most of it is now "dark" (unused) and probably always will be. Corporate acquisitions were funded at prices that fed on a volatile combination of ego and publicity, always pushing the next valuation further upwards. Thus, companies that were acquired for billions only a few months ago are, as result, worth literally pennies today.

Perhaps worst of all, licenses to offer "innovative" services were obtained at scandalous fees as, in some cases, governments chose to cash in on the feeding frenzy and sell tax-paying their corporate citizens down the river (not that those same citizens had the wit to raise any serious objections). Licenses, that is, for the right to sell almost entirely speculative services to a market in which no demand has been established, deploying an infrastructure and methodology to bill (and this make profits) which was at best embryonic and otherwise non-existent. It was the *Field of Dreams* scenario run amok: "Build it and they will come." We're still waiting for the 3G crowds to arrive, and a lot poorer for that.

Our story is, for all that, a human one. Its real protagonists are the investors who've lost their money, the retirees whose pension funds have been compromised, and the people, some of them friends, who've lost their jobs in the crash. It's not our intention to hide behind industry speak, insider terminology, or to write a "consultancy report" here. This will not be another faceless, earnest, business book (though there will be elements of that genre within these pages). We've come to feel that there's altogether too much demagoguery coming from inside the industry, too much "us" and "them", so to divide and conquer the unsuspecting public. Instead, this is just a general book about something that happened and is still happening now.

If you're an insider, you're an "expert" and you speak in the revered tones of one who's informed. You're allowed on a pedestal for that fact and thus your words are often taken at face value and believed. That's another element of this story: if you're going to play follow the leader, check out the leader first. Few in the primary and secondary worlds of telecoms bothered. And now everyone is paying the price.

Enough said. It is time for us to begin our account of *The Great Telecoms Scandal*, in our own words.

CHAPTER 1

A swindle exposed

The Great Telecoms Swindle emerges

On June 25th, 2002, WorldCom, Inc., "a leading provider of telecoms services globally" (*sic*), released the following statement:

Press Release: WorldCom Announces Intention to Restate 2001 and First Quarter 2002 Financial Statements

CLINTON, Miss., June 25, 2002 – WorldCom, Inc. (Nasdaq: WCOM, MCIT) today announced it intends to restate its financial statements for 2001 and the first quarter of 2002. As a result of an internal audit of the company's capital expenditure accounting, it was determined that certain transfers from line cost expenses to capital accounts during this period were not made in accordance with generally accepted accounting principles (GAAP). The amount of these transfers was $3.055 billion for 2001 and $797 million for first quarter 2002. Without these transfers, the company's reported EBITDA would be reduced to $6.339 billion for 2001 and $1.368 billion for first quarter 2002, and the company would have reported a net loss for 2001 and for the first quarter of 2002.

The company promptly notified its recently engaged external auditors, KPMG LLP, and has asked KPMG to undertake a comprehensive audit of the company's financial statements for 2001 and 2002. The company also notified Andersen LLP, which had audited the company's financial statements for 2001 and reviewed such statements for first quarter 2002, promptly upon discovering these transfers. On June 24, 2002, Andersen advised WorldCom that in light of the inappropriate transfers of line costs, Andersen's audit report on the company's financial statements for 2001 and Andersen's review of the company's financial statements for the first quarter of 2002 could not be relied upon.

The company will issue unaudited financial statements for 2001 and for the first quarter of 2002 as soon as practicable. When an audit is completed, the company will provide new audited financial statements for all required periods. Also, WorldCom is reviewing its financial guidance.

The company has terminated Scott Sullivan as chief financial officer and secretary. The company has accepted the resignation of David Myers as senior vice president and controller.

WorldCom has notified the Securities and Exchange Commission (SEC) of these events. The Audit Committee of the Board of Directors has retained William R. McLucas, of the law firm of Wilmer, Cutler & Pickering, former Chief of the Enforcement Division of the SEC, to conduct an independent investigation of the matter. This evening, WorldCom also notified its lead bank lenders of these events.

The expected restatement of operating results for 2001 and 2002 is not expected to have an impact on the Company's cash position and will not affect WorldCom's customers or services. WorldCom has no debt maturing during the next two quarters.

"Our senior management team is shocked by these discoveries," said John Sidgmore, appointed WorldCom CEO on April 29, 2002. "We are committed to operating WorldCom in accordance with the highest ethical standards."

"I want to assure our customers and employees that the company remains viable and committed to a long-term future. Our services are in no way affected by this matter, and our dedication to meeting customer needs remains unwavering," added Sidgmore. "I have made a commitment to driving fundamental change at WorldCom, and this matter will not deter the new management team from fulfilling our plans."

Actions to Improve Liquidity and Operational Performance

As Sidgmore previously announced, WorldCom will continue its efforts to restructure the company to better position itself for future growth. These efforts include:

Cutting capital expenditures significantly in 2002. We intend 2003 capital expenditures will be $2.1 billion on an annual basis.

Downsizing our workforce by 17,000, beginning this Friday, which is expected to save $900 million on an annual basis. This downsizing is primarily composed of discontinued operations, operations & technology functions, attrition and contractor terminations.

Selling a series of non-core businesses, including exiting the wireless resale business, which alone will save $700 million annually. The company is also exploring the sale of other wireless assets and certain South American assets. These sales will reduce losses associated with these operations and allow the company to focus on its core businesses.

Paying Series D, E and F preferred stock dividends in common stock rather than cash, deferring dividends on MCI QUIPS, and discontinuing the MCI tracker dividend, saving approximately $375 million annually.

Continuing discussions with our bank lenders.

Creating a new position of Chief Service and Quality Officer to keep an eye focused on our customer services during this restructuring.

"We intend to create $2 billion a year in cash savings in addition to any cash generated from our business operations," said Sidgmore. "By focusing on these steps, I am convinced WorldCom will emerge a stronger, more competitive player."

While the excrement had, figuratively, been hitting the ventilation extractor with alarming regularity across the telecoms sector in the preceding months as one established company after another lurched towards insolvency, when the WorldCom story broke the world (or at least the world of would-be "business experts") was suddenly willing to openly declare – and loudly – that the shit had well and truly hit the fan. Coming hot on the heels of the Enron crisis (with which the *dramatis personae* of the WorldCom saga shared a leading actor, the accounting firm Andersen), the telecoms market crash was transformed in a single stroke into the Great Telecoms Swindle.

SLEAZE AND MALFEASANCE

In the first instance, the story behind WorldCom's self-servingly phrased announcement was sleaze. As if the Enron implosion had not already been enough to make people mis-trust the ethics of the corporate world, here was proof positive that malfeasance was rife, that there was more than one bad apple in the pack. And, furthermore, whilst Enron was not a company in a market that most thought touched their own lives in a direct way, WorldCom was a key player in a market that in the preceding thirty-six months or so, had come to take centre stage in the worlds of investors and consumers alike through a combination of purported financial success and much-hyped technological progress.

Since the late 1990s, everywhere one turned, the talk was the telecoms sector. Money – much of it "our" money was invested via the equity markets in the form of stocks, pensions and other funds – into an industry that was almost too "hot" for its own good. Telecoms technology was in a state of revolution, and it was a revolution (honestly) from which the consumer was guaranteed to emerge a winner. 3G, broad-band, mobile, convergence . . . these were the themes from which all of us were about to benefit in ways we could only imagine, all released to endless profit through the benevolent effects of deregulation. It was "our" bank accounts that would, and briefly did, benefit first.

It turned out that, as with so many of history's great revolutions, many of the leaders of this one were as untrustworthy and incompetent as the extent that the visions they espoused were dramatic.

What WorldCom had actually announced in its press release amounted to the discovery and admission of a $3.7 billion accounting fraud. That's a lot of money and, in turn, prospectively an awful lot of fraud. What the company had done, in short, was to treat vast sums of cash (*sic*) that were actually expenses as capital expenditures, therefore allowing itself to report higher profits and more favourable cash flows than an honest accounting system would have permitted. The public, within hours, turned on this news with a vengeance.

WorldCom's announcement captured the popular imagination because of a combination of its scale, its timing, and the sheer effrontery of what its news represented. With stock markets already in recession, it was obvious that the economic downturn up to that point had not been fiercer simply because consumer spending had held up. Essentially, consumers had maintained their confidence in the economy in the belief that nothing was seriously wrong and a recession could be ridden out.

Suddenly, consumers were being given reasons (left, right, and center) to believe that their confidence might be badly misplaced. WorldCom, hot on the heels of Enron, suggested that a smell of rotten eggs was emanating from the boardroom; that the world of high finance and corporate leadership was rigged against investors by a clique of insiders who were either blind, stupid, or both. How could a multi-billion fraud catch anyone by surprise?

It took twenty-fours for the appropriate authority – the US Securities and Exchange Commission – to give their response to the events of the preceding day . . .

SEC Statement Concerning WorldCom

FOR IMMEDIATE RELEASE
2002–94

Washington, D.C., June 26, 2002 – The Securities and Exchange Commission issued the following statement today on WorldCom:

> The WorldCom disclosures confirm that accounting improprieties of unprecedented magnitude have been committed in the public markets.
>
> The public can be assured that we are actively investigating these and other events relating to the veracity of WorldCom's financial statements and disclosures. As part of that investigation, we are ordering the company to file, under oath, a detailed report of the circumstances and specifics of these matters.
>
> These events further demonstrate the need for comprehensive market regulatory reforms that the administration, the Congress, and the SEC have been advocating and implementing.

. . . by which time the cat was well and truly out of the bag. WorldCom had become a fully-fledged scandal on a truly global scale.

It didn't take long for US President George Bush to weigh in with his view, which finally removed the dire state of the telecoms market as a whole from being a "business page" issue to being a collapse worthy of international attention. WorldCom, and telecoms, were suddenly front page news and for reasons even worse than those which had brought the industry to the forefront in recent months. Prospective fraud provided the headlines and added oil to the fire, but as we shall see in the course of this book, the fire had been burning for some time already.

In the first instance, Bush (sounding suspiciously like a politician) described the news of WorldCom's activities as outrageous and promised that the people responsible would be held accountable. He added: "There is some concern about the validity of the balance sheet of corporate America and I can understand why. We've had too many cases of people abusing their responsibilities and people just need to know that the SEC is on it, our government is on it, and Arthur Andersen has been prosecuted. We will pursue, within our laws, those who are irresponsible." WorldCom, unlike Enron, was at least not peopled by the President's close Texan friends.

FROM CRASH TO SWINDLE

How could WorldCom, second to only AT&T in the long-distance market in the USA, a company which had grown from a small long-distance telco into a telecommunications force globally through more than 60 acquisitions in only 15 years hit the rocks in such spectacular fashion? How could an entire sector, in fact, appear to be falling apart all at once (albeit for reasons other than fraud)? Telecoms giants, only two years earlier the darlings of the investment community, lauded daily on the front pages of national newspapers as the heralds of a brave new commercial world that promised to benefit us all, were coming apart at the seams.

Once rock-solid corporate entities like Global Crossing, Lucent Technologies, Marconi, (to name but three) and others were now reduced to fighting tooth and nail for little more than survival in a scaled-down, severely distressed form. Others had vanished altogether. Even former monopolies like BT, Deutsche Telekom, and France Telecom were barely a step ahead of the plunge into such chaos. Shares that had twenty four months earlier sold for $50 or $100 were in many cases now trading for literally pennies. The very same advances that had promised to drive the telecoms sector to untold riches were proving in many ways to be its downfall. Something had gone dramatically wrong.

For telecoms, WorldCom was the event that put the icing on the cake and, for that matter, the cherry on the icing. The company's fall turned a crash into a swindle, and it turned the fear and dissatisfaction engendered by recession into sheer public contempt. In barely 20 years, WorldCom's history had run a course that had apparently taken it from the summit of industrial achievement to the depths of corporate depravity.

WORLDCOM'S ORIGINS

It had been as recently, in relative terms, as 1983 that two businessmen, Murray Waldron and William Rector, had sketched out a plan to create a discount long distance telecommunications provider called LDDS (Long-Distance Discount Service).

Within two years, an early investor, one Bernard Ebbers, had become the company's chief executive officer.

LDDS went public in 1989, through the acquisition of Advantage Companies Inc. and three years later expanded in an all-stock merger deal with discount long distance provider Advanced Telecommunications Corp. In 1993, the race for expansion that hallmarked the company's history was well and truly enjoined when LDDS acquired long distance providers Resurgens Communications Group Inc. and Metromedia Communications Corp. in a three-way stock and cash transaction that created the fourth-largest long-distance network in the United States. The company had arrived.

A year later, LDDS acquired domestic and international communications network IDB Communications Group Inc. in an all-stock deal and in 1995 voice and data transmission company Williams Telecommunications Group Inc. was added to the growing mix for $2.5 billion cash. At the same time, the company changed its name to name to WorldCom Inc.

Though the pace bordered on the frantic, Ebbers wasn't done. In 1996 WorldCom merged with MFS Communications Company Inc., which owned local network access facilities via digital fiber optic cable networks in and around major US and European cities, and UUNet Technologies Inc., an Internet access provider for businesses.

It was 1998 that, if it hadn't climbed the mountain in spectacular enough form already, WorldCom and, for that matter Ebbers, summitted. WorldCom completed three mergers: with

MCI Communications Corp. ($40 billion) – the largest merger in history at that time – with Brooks Fiber Properties Inc. ($1.2 billion) and with CompuServe Corp ($1.3 billion). Still not done, within twelve months WorldCom reached agreement with Sprint Corp, another telecoms giant, to merge.

In 2000, the US and European regulators drew the line, agreeing to block the proposed WorldCom/Sprint union which the companies then had no choice but to terminate. Undaunted, by 2001 Ebbers had architected a merger with Intermedia Communications Inc., a provider of data and Internet services to businesses.

Breathless growth doubtless had its distractions but perhaps reality began to set in on March 11, 2002 when WorldCom received a request for information from the US Securities and Exchange Commission (SEC) relating to accounting procedures and loans to its corporate officers. The questions provoked in that request were ultimately to send the upward spiral into a dizzying reverse which, in the end, proved even more dramatic than the climb.

THE TIDE TURNS

A month after the memo was sent, on April 3, WorldCom said it was cutting 3,700 jobs in the US or 6 percent of its staff, and 4 percent of its overall work force. The tide was slowly starting to turn, though with no sense of the impending tsunami that was then forming under the surface. Within two weeks, on April 22, more bad news had arrived: rating agency Standard & Poor's cut WorldCom's long-term and short-term corporate credit ratings. A day later Moody's Investors Service did the same, also slashing WorldCom's long-term ratings. As did a third such agency, Fitch, saying it expected WorldCom's revenue to deteriorate during 2002, with prospects for recovery in 2003 uncertain.

A week after that, on April 30, 2002 WorldCom CEO (and telecoms boom legend) Bernie Ebbers resigned with share prices slumping and an SEC probe of the company's support of his personal loans in progress. Vice Chairman John Sidgmore took up the reins in his place.

If the departure of the visible Ebbers was big news, in fact the real drama was just beginning to unfold. By early May, Moody's had cut WorldCom's long-term debt ratings to junk status, citing its deteriorating operating performance, debt and lowered expectations for further weakness.

Standard & Poor's followed suit within a day, also cutting WorldCom's credit rating to junk status and shortly thereafter removing WorldCom from its S&P 500 Index.

In a manner of speaking, WorldCom responded on May 15th, saying it would draw down a $2.65 billion bank credit line as it negotiated for a new $5 billion funding pact with its lenders. A week later and WorldCom said it would scrap dividend payments and eliminate its two tracking stocks, one that reflected its main Internet and data business and a second that reflected its residential long-distance telephone business.

Amidst the chaos of what we now know were the early days of the Swindle, lay small hints of what was to come. As it announced its first rounds of layoffs in April, WorldCom claimed that the SEC investigation into its books was not likely to be of grave concern. "The markets don't want to hear anything about accounting right now" in the post-Enron world, a spokesman said.

The importance of Wall Street's move to downgrade WorldCom was, even without the emergence of the Swindle, critical in hallmarking the sheer scale of the telecoms crisis. By downgrading short-term debt to junk status, the cost of borrowing for the US's second-largest long-distance carrier would significantly increase, meaning it would be difficult to effectively borrow at all. This would mean that WorldCom couldn't continue to run its business.

Within a matter of two months, a telecoms giant had been humbled. WorldCom's new chief executive, Sidgmore, told investors that the company had already renegotiated the one line of credit that would have been affected by the downgrade: $2 billion borrowed against its expectations of incoming revenue. Under a deal reached with banks, the company could borrow up to $1.5 billion based on incoming revenue and no longer faced credit-rating triggers that would require immediate repayment. "We don't see any impact on our bonds or bank credit facility," Sidgmore said during a conference call with investors.

Sidgmore also said the company planned to trim an additional $1 billion from its capital expenditure budget, which recently was reduced to $4.9 billion. That was bad news for companies such as Cisco Systems Inc. and Lucent Technologies Inc., which sell equipment to WorldCom.

WorldCom executives said that during the next several weeks they would look for more ways to cut spending and would consider selling assets. Among the assets that WorldCom might offer for sale were its relatively small mobile-phone business, Sidgmore said.

HUGE DEBTS LOADS – DECLINING REVENUES

In the 10 days after Ebbers left, Sidgmore and other executives met with employees and the company's 100 largest customers. "Mostly the message has been that they are nervous, but not nervous enough to switch," Sidgmore said of the customers. But Sidgmore also pointed out that customers had few options, given that most large telecommunications companies had huge debt loads amid declining revenue.

"All of these large carriers have had their ups and downs as well," he noted.

Then, on June 25th, came the crash. WorldCom's problems were not so manageable anymore.

Suddenly the company, and by extension the demise of the telecoms industry, was a multi-faceted front-page news story. It was a story about the failure of hype over expectation. It was a story of erstwhile glamour reduced to rubble, of the sort in which both journalists and their readers love to revel...the mighty humbled. It took the threads of the Enron scandal and proved that the problem of corporate ethics wasn't limited to the misbehaviour of a single company in a single market. It raised questions about industries and personalities, greed and contempt, technological progress and misjudgement. It gave the world – of investors and analysts alike – the chance to say "I told you so", as if they knew the apple was bad even though none of them had said anything before, whilst continuing to pour money into the telecoms abyss with no one holding a gun to their collective heads.

In a blame culture, suddenly everyone from the President to the man in the street had someone to blame. And Bernie Ebbers was target-in-chief, elected by common decree, and hauled before Congress to face the music almost overnight.

On Monday, July 8, to be exact.

CONGRESSIONAL CROCODILE TEARS

Give the world a manageably sized scandal and there's no mileage in devoting hours to researching the causes and addressing it in detail. Bring down a company the size of WorldCom and governments can be trusted to seize the opportunity to try to squeeze a few votes from atop the political soapbox. The same authorities who'd willingly presided – and taken the credit – for the booming telecoms market when times were good mercilessly reached for their rifles as would-be champions of a swindled public when the voters threatened to lose out. Through what one presumes were a welter of crocodile tears, a Congressional panel gathered in the first instance to question a key Wall Street analyst about his claim that he had no advance knowledge that WorldCom had improperly accounted for $3.9 billion in expenses.

Analysts, the *enfants terribles* of the Great Telecoms Swindle, providers of impartial (*sic*) advice for and on behalf of the financial industry, into the activities of whose key clients that advice was designed to judge. To put it bluntly, the financial industry (in this case represented by investment bankers) figuratively makes money by engaging in activities comparable to selling cars to the public and advising the carmakers themselves at the same time and, with a straight face, it claims to offer the former group of clients an impartial evaluation of the abilities of the latter group of (bigger) clients. Who'd have thought it? Yet, before the Swindle emerged, no one had apparently thought to make much of a fuss about the existence of such a clearly misconceived hierarchy before. For which retrospective pent-up fury, one Jack Grubman was to carry the can. A fall guy if ever there was one.

Grubman was an analyst at Salomon Smith Barney, and he was to become famous overnight in the worst possible way. It was he, with his "close ties" to WorldCom, who had downgraded his rating of the company's stock (to "underperform") only a few days before the Swindle was announced. For his troubles, Grubman was ordered to appear – under subpoena – before the US House of Representatives Financial Services Committee, along with several WorldCom officials.

His supporting cast included Ebbers, Scott D. Sullivan, WorldCom's former chief financial officer, and David Myers, a former controller, in what amounted to a three-ring circus. All were expected to decline to answer any questions and thus to prospectively incriminate themselves, sheltering instead under the Fifth Amendment of the US constitution.

On June 26, the SEC had charged WorldCom in New York federal court with defrauding investors. According to the action, through irregular accounting methods that had started in 2001, the company had been enabled to appear profitable when in fact it was not. The charges were expected to be the first of many, as WorldCom and its officers were the subject of numerous ongoing investigations conducted by multiple federal agencies.

Grubman himself had denied claims that he knew about WorldCom's accounting irregularities before the crash. In testimony given to the committee the weekend before the hearings, he'd said that such speculations was "categorically false" and that his downgrade of the company's rating was based solely on public information. Congress was less than willing to believe him, the committee claiming to have copies of an email sent from one of his associates to WorldCom's Sullivan that indicated at least some knowledge of the situation before it exploded into the public view. The email, sent on June 24th, asked specifically about rumours concerning a $3 billion charge because of accounting problems. Twenty-four hours later, WorldCom had gone nuclear.

HOW INDEPENDENT ARE THE ANALYSTS?

Grubman had hitherto been WorldCom's Wall Street champion analyst, talking up the stock through both the thick and the thin of recent years.

As an analyst, he was supposed to be objective, yet the minutes of an October, 1999 meeting suggest that he was brought in to advise the WorldCom board on a potential merger, a highly unusual activity for an "independent" analyst to engage in.

The committee extended its interest by asking two additional players in the unfolding drama to appear: former Andersen partner Melvin Dick, who was in charge of auditing WorldCom's financial statements; and WorldCom's chairman, Bert C. Roberts. Setting out the parameters of the investigation, the committee made the depth of the WorldCom drama clear. For a start, they wanted to know was the scandal limited to the period already made public, or were other accounting issues involved? WorldCom had already admitted that its own investigation was extending into possible problems in 1999 and 2000.

Furthermore, Congressional investigators were trying to uncover whether WorldCom had over-billed its customers by as much as $3 billion in recent years. Plus, the now almost obligatory questions about bonuses given to the company officers, in particular $10 million given to Sullivan, fired in the aftermath of the scandal breaking yet still in receipt of a payoff that had been contingent on his remaining an employee through to the end of 2002. WorldCom had already filed a claim of its own to recover the amount.

Hearings the following day yielded few surprises. Both Ebbers and Sullivan, as expected, refused to testify, invoking their right against self-incrimination. Other witnesses answered questions, but shed little light on who might be responsible for the meltdown at WorldCom. If the committee achieved anything, however, it was to expose in broad daylight the snug (and smug) cartel between accountants, investment bankers, and corporate officers – now the target for Congressional reform – that was seen to plague corporate America and, indeed, the broader corporate world.

Grubman's responses invoked outrage, as he testified to his closeness to WorldCom, socializing with Ebbers and others and on three occasions attending closed meetings with the company's board. Melvin Dick, the former manager for Arthur Andersen, offered the doubtful testimony that an auditor could only depend on the figures he was given to work with in the first place.

Ebbers did himself little good, taking the Fifth whilst simultaneously denying that he was in any way complicit in the scandal personally, a claim which lead members of the committee to suggest he had waived his right to self-incrimination and as a result that he should be held in contempt of Congress. Observed one Representative, Barney Frank: "All the people who are supposed to be checking each other are in fact collaborating with each other."

Grubman's disclosures about his relationship with WorldCom did him no favours. Claiming that in attending meetings with the board, he was there only to provide "colour" and advice about how the market might react to WorldCom entering certain transactions, Representative Frank pointed out that those were reactions that Grubman would help to shape. Grubman's firm did much of the investment banking for the actual deals, and had made millions in fees for their work over the preceding years. Grubman could only add: "I am saddened that people lost money, I am saddened that people lost jobs. . . . In hindsight I regret that I was wrong in rating WorldCom highly for too long."

He also strongly denied that he aware of the impending earnings restatement in advance, in spite of the fact that the committee held emails indicating that one of Grubman's colleagues had desperately tried to contact WorldCom on June 24th to address rumours of major accounting problems. That didn't stop the same colleague reporting to bondholders that day that they should not be worried by Grubman's downgrading of WorldCom the previous week.

In the absence of either Ebbers or WorldCom willingly assuming their places in the firing line, it fell to the bit players to take the brunt of the committees attack, in particular Andersen which had already been at the heart of the Enron scandal. Putting it succinctly, "You were General Custer and WorldCom were the Indians, and you got slaughtered," said New York Republican Sue W. Kelly.

Andersen was asked whether they had requested journal entries from WorldCom officials to document the numbers with which they had been presented, and replied that they had not. They did claim to have asked for "top-side entries," or notations of accounting handled outside normal company practice, and were told there were none.

CREATIVE ACCOUNTING

Further developments broke soon after the first round of hearings. Sullivan claimed that he had told Ebbers about the creative accounting practices that had made WorldCom look much healthier than it in fact was, though Ebbers, through his lawyer, denied the claim. This was uncovered by the house committee and, said one Representative, it was "the first evidence that he [Ebbers] was in fact aware of the cooking of the books." Ebbers' lawyers predicatably disputed the claim, saying he didn't "know anything about Scott Sullivan's decision to reallocate expenses on WorldCom's balance sheets."

The committee meanwhile started to receive the physical evidence in the form of five boxes of documents that it had subpoenaed from WorldCom. These revealed that since early 2001, Sullivan had been classifying operating expenses as capital expenditures, allowing WorldCom to spread costs over several years instead of accounting for them immediately. According to Sullivan, he had made Ebbers aware that "hundreds of millions of dollars" were being shifted in this way. Sullivan also claimed that he believed that, in so doing, he was following proper accounting practice though both Andersen and KPMG, WorldCom's new auditor, found the actions to violate accepted accounting principles.

At the same time, new WorldCom chief executive Sidgmore acknowledged the likelihood that the company would file for bankruptcy as it attempted to reorganize its finances. The company, he said, was already looking for assets to sell and would close certain unprofitable businesses outright if buyers could not be found. He added, "We cannot predict at this time what will happen to our common shareholders – we are still reviewing all of our options. The main goal is to keep the company intact and to provide service to our customers." No music for the ears of at least one group of Swindle victims.

Another victim group, former WorldCom employees who had been laid off as a result of the crash, filed a motion at US District Court asking for a temporary restraining order that would allow them to collect severance pay without agreeing to forgo future legal action against the company. WorldCom had told them they would get no money if they did not sign a form to that effect, which the company said was the standard severance agreement that had been in use for years.

WORLDCOM FILES FOR BANKRUPTCY

On Monday August 22nd, the first round in the Great Telecoms Swindle was completed when WorldCom announced that it had filed for bankruptcy protection, the largest filing in US history. It listed its assets as $107 billion, and said it did not have the cash to pay interest on more than $30 billion of debt. WorldCom claimed it would be able to maintain service to its customers because of a credit line secured by the bankruptcy filing, and that it also had enough money to operate and pay its employees for at least one year. The filing, Sidgmore explained, would enable the company to reorganize and move forward.

He also insisted that WorldCom would emerge from bankruptcy with a clean balance sheet and effectively free of debt. This would be achieved by reducing costs and selling non-core assets.

The spectacular events affecting one company in late spring

and early summer 2002 were, however, far from the first stages in a chain of events that had been taking shape for some years, only to spiral out of control and onto the public's radar screen much, much later. The WorldCom swindle was, in fact, little more than the icing on a much bigger and more complex cake. In the greater scheme of the telecoms market crash (which had, of course, brought down WorldCom alongside many other market leaders), the reality was that the swindle provided a convenient peg on which headline writers could hang, or attempt to hang, their stories. These were stories the genesis of which long preceded the events of late spring and early summer, 2002.

In fact, the swindle at WorldCom was largely a reaction to market forces that had shaped the telecoms industry over a period of approximately twenty years or longer. These forces in many ways helped to cause what happened at WorldCom, rather than the swindle being in any way causally related to the crash itself. That is not to excuse the swindle, for a swindle is what it was, but it is to say that various events created a fertile ground for malfeasance to take place, as we shall see in the course of this book. With or without malfeasance, the bursting of the telecoms bubble was almost inevitable.

Look at this way. The telecoms industry in the 1980s and to an even greater extent the 1990s resembled a wave upon which surfer after surfer had hopped on for a ride. As the wave swelled and became more exciting, new surfers joined, many of whom – in their arrogance – were blissfully unaware of the fact that barely knew how to surf and were thus all too poorly prepared for the unconsidered eventuality that nature might send the wave crashing beyond their control. And when the wave did turn – into a tsunami – this lack of planning was exposed. A lot of the surfers went under, some clung (and are still clinging) to the surface, gasping for life, and others, perhaps unsurprisingly, chose unedifying methods in an attempt to keep their heads above water. Almost no one, it turned out, was surfing on a board up to the job though the few that were are the companies who will still be around when the market eventually rebounds (as it one day will).

This book is to some extent about the wave, because if we fail to understand that then the Swindle itself makes little sense at all. It would become, in that case, the story of one bad apple isolated from all the others in the barrel and that, in reality, is not the WorldCom story at all. Make no mistake, there was a bad apple but nothing will be learned from its existence if we make no attempt to understand the conditions that caused it go bad.

We will look at the major forces that turned the wave into a tsunami, all of which, in many ways came to a head more or less at once. Because so much revolutionary change occurred in a short space of time, the demands on telecoms businesses evolved at an almost unprecedented rate and meant that companies long versed in their set business methods needed to reinvent themselves, re-engineer their models, and restructure their networks almost overnight.

IGNORANCE AND INCOMPETENCE

The real Swindle, as we shall see, was how poorly equipped many of the CEOs of these companies were for the job. Questions should most certainly be asked with regard to WorldCom's specific and brazen actions, but many, many more should be asked about how such widespread ignorance and incompetence could take root in the offices of CEOs and the boardrooms of so many companies. How could one industry have such a universal crisis in leadership at a single time? In fact, we will later note how some CEOs did lead their companies competently through the minefield yet their companies are now paying a price in the financial markets because they are tarred with the same brush as their competitors who went under.

Before we rejoin WorldCom and the crisis-strewn telecoms market of today, though, we must start by putting the Swindle into perspective.

CHAPTER 2

Into the breach

From POTS to the next generation world

There was a time not very ago when the telecoms market was a reasonably straightforward place in which to do business. Its service offering was the connection of voice calls through a medium known as Plain Old Telephone Service (POTS). The business of telecoms was largely transacted by monopolistic public utilities, one in each country, and these organizations in very simple terms were (like a lot of monopolies) pretty good at what they did (which in this case was fundamentally network engineering) and not very good at servicing their customers (who were, after all, a captive audience so there was no need to be particularly good at that). As telecoms, like other utilities but unlike other industries, has a geopolitical impact and therefore responsibility, it could be argued that this set-up made a certain amount of sense.

Telecoms services were pretty straightforward. The network and the network elements needed to make things work were long-established, reliable, and functional. They could be refined by advances like new and improved signalling systems but, as the reader will know, over the last twenty years for the most part when you've picked up a phone and dialled the requisite number, your call has been completed without a problem. If not always like clockwork, things worked. You made your calls, got your monthly bill, paid it, and that was telecoms – at least as far as the consumer was concerned

Then, mainly in the course of the 1980s, things started to change. In fact, a lot of far-reaching change in just about every corner of the telecoms universe was imposed on the market almost all at once. What happened wasn't so much a revolution, as about half a dozen revolutions occurring at the same time or, at any rate, hot on the heels of each other.

DISMANTLING THE OLD MONOPOLIES

First, the cosy, traditional monopolistic world was dismantled (some would say in a self-defeating manner). Then, the traditional voice telephone call was deemed to be the industry's past rather than its future. That lay with an entirely new sort of service, data. This meant that half a century's worth of network building would at some point become redundant because the network required to carry data was entirely different to the wires-in-the-ground required to carry voice. Which meant, in turn, that new networks had to be built.

At the same time as these changes were coming onto the radar screen, what amounted to an entirely new telecoms market – mobile – exploded into life in the most spectacular way possible, a sea change in the way the industry managed itself and the way the consumer related to it. What drove the initial mobile explosion was really pent-up demand. Conceptually, the notion of a portable version of fixed line telephony service had always held considerable appeal to the public but until the late 1980s and early 1990s, the enabling technology for mass market mobile had not caught up with the prospective market itself. When it did, a boom was inevitable and once voice mobile became ubiquitous, various social dynamics (such as the popularity of SMS amongst specific demographic groups) quickly propelled the market even further ahead, outstripping even its own optimistic expectations.

Also simultaneously, the barriers to the internationalization of the telecoms market were brought down. The world of telecoms, in the space of perhaps ten short years, could be hallmarked by the phrase "all change, all at once".

In the beginning, before liberalization, before everything changed, and before the Great Telecoms Swindle was even a twinkle in anyone's eye, the global telecoms market was, as we said, a pretty straightforward place. Incumbent operators were largely self-reliant and uncomplicated organizations (albeit unwieldy ones) and, as monopolies had no competition from which to distinguish either themselves or their service offerings nor any great need to develop as organizations responsive either to the end user of services or to the conditions that prevail in a free market.

The monopolies owned both the physical networks (essentially copper wires in the ground) and the customers, with total control over the critical "local loop", the last network mile between the local exchange and the customer's home access to which, in recent years, has been such a competitive battleground post-liberalization. Phone companies were largely faceless – which is to say that they weren't marketing organizations because they didn't need to be – and the functionality and progressive aspect of their services was limited because, the natural science of progress aside, no moving force existed to drive the market forward.

The technological world of telecoms was, in a relative sense, equally simple. Making a voice phone call over a fixed line network involved the reservation of a single, unique circuit on which no other activity could be transacted for the duration of that call. Phone companies made their money on the basis of the number of calls made, their duration, and the distance they travelled. All the hardware and software elements required to enable and account for this were in place, and were proven to work.

THE DATA SERVICES REVOLUTION

The arrival of data services in the 1990s, allied to the birth of the competitive carrier market spawned by liberalization, revolutionized the equation, as we shall see in this book, on both the network engineering and the economic sides of the equation. It required a fundamental change in both the nature of the telephone company (newcomers, who had no legacy of incumbency to shake off probably had a built-in advantage here) and also a radical change in the design of the network.

In recent years, data traffic has outstripped voice traffic over telephone networks by ever greater margins. This has meant that the barriers that once existed between the world of the Internet and the world of the PSTN (Public Switched Telephone Network – essentially, the "old world") have necessarily disappeared. Giant global phone companies have invested heavily in broadband networks that deploy what the industry terms "next generation" technology.

Why? The fundamental reason is competition. In a free market, competing players need to broaden and differentiate the services they offer from those of their competitors. With the growth of the Internet and the boom in data, operators have had to literally (in some cases) almost re-engineer their businesses from the ground up.

In the early 1990s and before, the main source of revenue for the telephone company was, as noted, fixed line telephony. That is to say, voice calls made via wires in the ground. First generation networks, as they are known, used circuit switching technology utilizing analogue signalling for the completion of calls.

As both market liberalization and the mobile boom took hold, second generation networks evolved, still circuit switched but utilizing digital signalling. As a result of this, and the need for ever greater quantities of data to be conveyed across the network, a sea change was made to deploy what is known as "packet switching". This is the basic technology that is the axis on which the next generation network rests.

Particularly for the former monopolies (or incumbents, as they are known within the telecoms market) the challenge of migration from the circuit switched to first a hybrid and ultimately the pure next generation network, has been and remains considerable.

It was for the reasons above amongst others that the ground shifted significantly not only for the telcos themselves, but also in the massive secondary telecoms equipment market at the same time. The changes in the physical network created demand for a whole new roster of products to enable and support the new network's technology, and of this demand the Cisco legend in particular was to a great extent born. New "next generation" equipment suppliers sprung up like mushrooms, moving apace from the drawing board to wildly successful IPOs in many cases, and long-established players in the circuit switched equipment market fell behind at their peril (we all know, and in any event we shall later discuss in detail, what happened at Lucent).

The newly formed competitive carriers entering the market sought to rapidly deploy IP networks, essentially bypassing the first generation network in the process, and many of these players saw little reason to make any significant investment in circuit switching equipment at all. The circuit switched standard was both expensive and unwieldy whereas the Internet Protocol (IP) network was less expensively and more rapidly deployed.

TECHNOLOGICAL CHALLENGES

For the long-established giants and former incumbents already possessed of substantial circuit switched networks, the challenge was both different and greater. On the one hand, with switches themselves costing millions of pounds, none were about to simply write off legacy investments and leap blindly into the future but all had to recognize the need to migrate towards IP hybrid networks at least. This need gave birth to another lucrative arm of the equipment market, that of building the technologies that made the transition possible such as media gateways and IP integrated switches. Ovum, the consultancy, projected the value of that market to be $1.3 billion by 2006.

Why the shift in technology? Without wishing to bog the reader down in detail, the voice and data unified next generation network is based on the aforementioned IP, which was originally used to interconnect the networks that formed the Internet itself. As opposed to the circuit switched network, where the completion of a call (*sic*) requires the reservation of a single circuit, in IP networks data is transmitted as a stream of packets which are routed via the IP addresses of every computer using the protocol. As the Internet has become more and more widely used, IP has become ever more ubiquitous.

IP has a number of significant advantages over the switched network that, from an economic and market perspective made its widespread adoption inevitable. It is, first and foremost, an open standard, with no proprietary ownership. Packet switching, at its core, is faster and less expensive than circuit switching and, furthermore, packet switched networks can be scaled (expanded) more easily and rapidly. As mentioned above, equipment costs are significantly lower meaning both purchase and operational savings for the service provider. IP networks are also more flexible in what they can carry, meaning that value-added services (those other than voice) can more easily be developed and offered to the customer. This was, at the time, particularly important in light of the expected boom in first e-commerce and then m- (mobile) commerce.

In short, the expectation was (and to a great extent still is) for the unified network to both simplify the world of telecoms infrastructure and, possibly even more importantly, to enable the emergence of new applications. This would allow phone companies, in the traditional sense, to stop being phone companies and rather to respond freely and flexibly to market conditions through an ongoing process of innovation. Suddenly, the telecoms world would have value, rather than price, as the basis of competition. In short, once again, all change.

The challenge facing the telecoms market had thus been revolutionized by the 1990s. So many balls were bouncing (in the equipment, services, network, and other related worlds) that it is little wonder that some eyes were taken off some of them some of the time (though the lie has been given comprehensively to the once held image of statesmanlike chief executives intelligently and with restraint plotting a safe course through changing market conditions). Suddenly, rather than simply sending out bills and collecting revenues, competition in telecoms was about service innovation, individualization (giving the customer what he or she wants) and, to a lesser extent, service bundling or convergence which, in an integrated network, was suddenly possible.

If your first impression in absorbing the preceding paragraphs is to imagine that from a business perspective, to arrive at a critical juncture in time in which new, cheaper technology, the potential for new products all based on an open standard, and proceeding under increasingly liberalized market conditions was akin to arriving in the land of milk and honey, you'd probably be sharing the same view held by many of the market's key officers at the time (an awful lot of whom are not working in the positions they held then today).

At each turning there appeared to be endless opportunity, each day brought grandiose claims of "world's first" innovations (although it turned out that was rarely enough actually the case), and in the race to cash in no one apparently saw the wood for the trees. It was, in fact, the sheer lack of restraint, introspection, or measured analysis from chief executives who should have know much, much, better that originally convinced us personally that sometime, somewhere, things were bound to go horribly wrong. Put very simply, to quote the old finance industry maxim, if it sounds too good to be true, it almost certainly *is* too good to be true.

TOO MUCH STYLE; TOO LITTLE SUBSTANCE

To give a flavour of those times, though, really is to describe what appeared to be a land of milk and honey. The expense account largesse of an industry whose collective bank account looked like a one-way passage to riches for all distracted not only the market itself but, apparently, many of those who looked in on it as analysts and commentators from the fringes. Here's a technology stock, here's a "buy" recommendation. The environment was sometimes Gekko-esque. We fondly remember the least glamorous company we have ever come across, essentially peopled by a group of flat-capped software engineers, launching a new product release in an art-deco London hotel amidst an ocean of canapés and looking, for all the world, utterly ridiculous in the process. That their release was surrounded by as much style and as little substance as their choice of hotel betrayed the weakness inherent in its foundations, though no one apparently cared to notice.

As we've noted, in some ways too much was happening at once. New technologies rarely come into existence as the finished article and, furthermore, more new technologies are often needed to enable them to work. These, too, have to be developed. Then they have to be sold, and if they're sold on the premise that they're the key to greater future profits, then that promise has to be realized if they're to be paid for retrospectively. For that to happen, in very simple terms you have to know what to do with the new technology (as well as to ensure that it actually works and it's desirable in and of itself) once you've got it. Few of the players across the telecoms market were truly equipped to sensibly pursue the steps, and answer the questions, above.

The equipment market, in many ways the real evangelists who led the industry into the pit, sold the brave new world to the telcos who in turn sold it to the consumer, confidently on the surface but with increasing worry underneath. They saw opportunity and cashed in, but in the process did so in many cases by funding their sales. The telcos who bought the equipment were, it turned out, effectively unable to capitalize on it (certainly in the short term) and in turn, over the course of the late nineties, delivered a lot of promise unmatched by products to the customer. What happened next was inevitable. Consumers lost confidence in the brave new world. And payments were missed all the way down the chain.

Still, for all the evangelizing and inflated sales pitches from the equipment market, liberalization had given the telcos a challenge that they needed the next generation network to meet. The problem wasn't that the future had necessarily been envisioned wrongly so much as it hadn't arrived manageably and it hadn't arrived, as whole, in good working order.

THE NEED FOR SERVICE INNOVATION

The competitive telco, unlike its incumbent predecessor, had to maintain and increase its revenues and to do so the battle for the customer was enjoined. For the first time in history, telcos had to understand and interact with the consumers that used their services, thereby retaining existing clients and attracting new ones (the basis of growth in any industry). It could, of course, in part do this the old way (by reducing tariffs on existing services) but that would not prove to be enough. In order to differentiate itself within an increasingly populous environment, the new competitive carrier had to innovate. Innovation was (and remains) a challenge on two levels. First, external innovation in the form of new products and services and secondly, and perhaps even more importantly, internal innovation which is to say managing the transition to becoming a new type of business.

Furthermore, the basic rule of an expanding operator market and demand for innovative services by the consumer lead to the belief that there would be a need for dramatically increased capacity within the network. On what proved to be vastly misjudged estimates of how great that capacity needed to be, companies like WorldCom became, briefly, major players as mile upon mile of fibre was laid to ready the world for an explosion that was never to come.

Exactly what service innovation will amount to is still a matter, in spite of what some may claim, for speculation. Only the fact of oncoming change itself is certain. The pace and the nature of it remain an open question. At a minimum the successful telco in future must support standard services (voice calls, email, web access) and thereafter the challenge is to discover what works from within a broad church of potential options.

These might include "infotainment" services offered over the Internet, financial services, personal management services, location-based services and more. It was visions of this future that lead to the re-shaping in some cases of the broader business landscape itself, with the merger of AOL and Time Warner (since disbanded) being the obvious example of a partnership made with an eye firmly on this mooted change. That the two had few synergies and the union apparently rapidly fell into a state of ineffectiveness again speaks volumes about the how the publicity surrounding the revolution outstripped the market realities inherent within it.

Some of the problems should have been obvious from the start. In the average customer's mind, for instance, the Internet is associated with free or very cheap services. It was always questionable to what extent this would remain the case with new, more advanced services though that fact seems to have dissuaded few in anticipating their likely popularity. Furthermore, the likelihood is that futuristic, next generation services will not remain so simple. Yet the telecoms industry has little experience, and has proven ineffective to date in its ability to explain why and how, regardless, such advances benefit the customer. Even in a competitive market the industry remains, on the whole, more comfortable talking about technology than customer service. Most of all, telcos still have little sense of self as entities in the wider commercial world. Not only are they often (though not always) less than customer focused (particularly at the top end of the market) but many conduct internecine divisional warfare within their own walls. There are "fixed" divisions and "mobile" divisions, "voice" divisions and "data" divisions and so on, each with its own agenda, few forming a lithe and responsive entirety to cope with a demanding new market.

TECHNOLOGICAL TRANSFORMATION

Thus in a relatively short span of time was the telecoms market transformed from a technological perspective. From offering a limited, highly reliable voice service over a long-proven network backbone deploying familiar and established technologies via, at the start, a relative handful of large telephone companies twenty odd years ago, by the end of the century everything had changed to the extent that the playing field was unrecognizable. Radical new advances in technology, changes in standards, a revolution in the very nature of the business had taken hold. On all sides of the coin, from the equipment providers to the business and operational support players to the telcos themselves there was a frantic scramble to secure a piece of the profit pie for which few appeared to know the recipe or the ingredients for success. The telecoms customer sat by, at first pouring money into the action in the form of investments on the strength of the message and the promise but, as time went on and not much happened in the form of deliverables, increasingly bemused.

In essence, this market transformation journey represents one of the roads that ends at the juncture we've called the Great Telecoms Swindle, the present crash itself. Running parallel to this road is another of equal importance . . . the path of liberalization or deregulation through which the industry went in the corresponding period in time, during the 1980s and 1990s. It is to that path that we now turn our attention.

CASE STUDY

NTL

Barclay Knapp, founder and chief executive of the cable company NTL, Inc., sits comfortably in the pantheon of once iconic telecoms market leaders. His company, like so many others, soared high and crashed equally spectacularly, though happily without the spotlight of the Swindle itself descending on its activities. Which is to say no corruption exposed . . . just (*sic*) incompetence, once again, on a truly heroic scale.

NTL, in a by now all too familiar story, managed to borrow US$17.5 billion to fund its aggressive expansion program in the boom years (1998–2000), expenditure which yielded few tangible results and even fewer of them good ones. By early 2002, the money-men were demanding answers to the question of what had happened to their investment.

In a short space of time, accelerated as telecoms players fell out favour in the financial markets, NTL's shares fell from almost $110 to just 43¢, heralding the possibility of a collapse of WorldCom-like proportions. Once again, as we have suggested throughout this book, investors might want to start their quest to find someone to blame in front of the mirror. NTL leadership was ineffectual, to be sure, but it is they, in their misguided quest for "can't miss returns", who effectively created the conditions that enabled NTL and Knapp to destroy their investment.

NTL by tradition was never a run-of-the-mill company. Listed in New York, it was owned and run by Americans yet sought to establish itself in Europe, a geography where Knapp had identified an underdeveloped cable sector which afforded significant opportunity. Knapp's vision was to create a cable giant and he persuaded the financial markets to underwrite it.

In the last two years of the 1990s NTL spent in the region of $20 billion on 21 acquisitions spread across the continent, and the resulting company became the Europe's largest cable operator with five million customers. Knapp proposed that NTL would offer digital television, telecoms services, and broadband and Internet access to its customers, in so doing including more or less every "hot" industry in the next generation age under its umbrella. For financiers with money, at the time, to burn, it was almost a can't-miss proposition. Get involved in any one of those markets and the funding would be there, but all three at once. No one could resist (and thus, no one bothered to ask many questions about whether NTL could deliver on its promises, either).

The irony now is that NTL should have been a can't-miss proposition, too. Britain, for one, was a sitting duck for exploitation by a canny cable operator. But in his desire to sprint before his company could crawl, Knapp plunged NTL headlong over a cliff. What should have been healthily growing revenues found it impossible to keep up with and support the requirements of constant expansion. The ability of NTL to generate cash was insufficient as its ever increasing capital expenditures burnt through all the money it had available. Just doing well, in the face of Knapp's business plans, would never be doing well enough.

With a financial position engendered by such imbalances, the fall of the company was inevitable and, when the greater telecoms market collapsed even its one obvious way out was cut off. Asset sales became impossible as the market for telecoms properties disappeared almost overnight. NTL could even not raise the money it needed to meet cash flow commitments through a fire sale.

By early 2000 its only way to survive was a restructuring of debt and an extensively revamped business plan, proposals for which saw the once breezily confident Knapp faced with the prospect of eating a healthy dose of humble pie (an act imminently more appealing than testifying before a Congressional committee, it must be said).

NTL's biggest shareholder, France Telecom (with its own debt related problems in tow) wanted out and its other major investor, the US giant Verizon Communications wasn't showing much interest in propping up Knapp's empire, either. Suggestions were that the reasons for this reluctance were simple: basically, NTL neither did nor ever had known what it was doing. It had viscerally failed to complete the most elementary course in cable company management. To paraphrase a former US president, it spoke loudly, and carried a very little stick indeed.

The problems? High churn rates (customer turnover . . . NTL was constantly losing more existing customers than it was bringing in new ones) and low penetration rates were the primary ingredients for the mess. A company that can neither attract nor keep customers clearly isn't deploying a formula for any kind of success, long term or otherwise. Furthermore, a great many of the customers NTL did have were vociferously unhappy with the service they received, creating a poor image of the company in the markets in which it competed. In short, NTL may have had a great story, but it appeared to have no idea whatsoever how to make it come true. All the while investors sat on the sidelines and watched passively while their investment imploded.

For its part, NTL's public messages during this period have become the stuff of telecoms Swindle legend and never mind a forensic examination of the evidence, even a cursory review of its statements during the boom make tragic-comic reading today. It described, for instance, 2001 as being a period for "getting down to business", after reporting a pre-tax loss of more than $3 billion in 2000.

Stephen Carter, managing director of NTL in the UK, said at the time "we will be digesting the activity (acquisitions) of 2000. We are now a business of scale, with customers and strong products." None of which, history suggests, they had any idea what to do with.

As was proved, in May 2002, when NTL filed for bankruptcy protection as part of a plan to put the company back on a sound financial footing. According to documents supporting the filing in New York, the company had assets of US$16.8 billion and debts of $23.4 billion, largely related to its spending spree and its inability to service the resultant debt as the equity markets crashed.

When the bankruptcy filing was entered, NTL had already begun its financial overhaul when a group of leading creditors agreed to swap over $10 billion of debt for a controlling share in the company. This move, which alleviated a large portion of the crippling debt burden hindering the company, was one of the biggest corporate defaults ever recorded. The bankruptcy filing sought to protect NTL from its remaining creditors while the restructuring plan was worked out and focussed on a new business plan that would divide the company into two firms, once focussed on the UK and Ireland and the other on NTL's interest in continental Europe.

NTL continues to operate under bankruptcy protection at the time of writing, though it is expected to emerge from the process soon after the restructuring efforts are completed.

The last word on NTL should go to the two groups of people on whom any company ought best to be able to rely to provide an accurate reference: employees and customers. There is a near-legendary website that exposes the real extent of the mess Knapp and his associates have made and thus from NTLHellworld we quote the following:

> I actually work for NTL and at the moment, morale is very low and each person in the customer service is fed up and disenfranchised at the moment. According to some of the comments on the site, we are all bad, should be closed down and are incompetent. We work

long hours, are tied to a headset and stats are gathered into everything we do. A lot of us would love to give good customer service but do not have the management remit to allow us do so. There are changes in procedures and nothing in place to assist us in the change. There will be soon a grading of CSAs but this has been daubed degrading of csas. It is seen as a money saving exercise. Everything is on the cheap at the moment and there is great demoralisation in the camp. Please spare a thought for us as we try to do an excellent job but do not have the resources to do a good job.

A lot of us are looking for other jobs and it galls that good agents have left the company and gone elsewhere. So you are left with the inexperienced people and not given to the experienced – The last two rounds of redundancies have hit us very badly. I have studied management and am a member of the Institute of Management but that does not count for anything. We let good people go without actualising them into the best place for thier experience and expertise. The only thing that management can do to "try to chivvy us up" is to hand out children's sweets and patronise us.

Please spare a thought for us, we would like to do a good job if we had the remit.

* * *

I had nothing but trouble with NTL from the time I moved to Nuneaton and a house with an NTL line.

Payments not credited to my phone bill, Internet access cut off after a year of use because I had the wrong type of line, never watched the digital TV because it was rubbish.

The only thing that they managed to get right was coming round on the right day to pick up the box because I disconnected and went back to BT.

I've had problems with the following:

1. It took 5 months to get a final statement confirming all bills were paid from them. Without this I could not get my £700 deposit for my rented house.
2. It took 4 months to get my NTL World CD.
3. They randomly cut of our phone line and it took 2 weeks to get it back.
4. Loss of digital TV for 3 weeks.
5. Hours spent listening to 8 bars of 'music' on hold over and over.
6. Phoned 3 times to have Film 4 removed and info sent on new channel packs. Recieved: Loss of All our channels and 3 sets of info on film 4!
7. Delivery of cable modem: 3 weeks late and unreliable service supplied by it.
8. I'm no longer put on hold but told to phone back later.
9. Threat of disconnection for non-payment; but they didn't set up the direct debit and I can't get though to their accounts department.
10. Ntl interactive only causes the TV to crash.

To summarise, I hope NTL burn, slowly and painfully in the deepest and darkest part of hell I can find for them. (And hopefully fairly soon).

CHAPTER 3

The floodgates open

A potted overview of telecoms deregulation

That the telecoms market presently bears more than a passing resemblance to a multi-car pile up is a fact with which few are inclined to argue. The question that needs to be asked and the answers that must be understood if either a way out of the present malaise is to be found or, alternatively, if any lessons are to be learned from the experience is this: how did the industry arrive in the situation in which it now finds itself? Why has the crash occurred and could it have been avoided?

Inevitably, the story behind the headlines is more complex than the headlines themselves. Mismanagement and fraud, blind optimism and incompetence (often on an almost heroic scale) – some or all of which have been on display – make great newspaper copy. Reality, however, is never quite as straightforward. We used the analogy of a multi-car pile pile-up advisedly. A lot of cars were involved and the role of each one has to be considered if, in turn, we are to make any sense of the greater accident itself.

Perhaps the first car to arrive at ground zero (the crash site) and thus the starting point in what has turned out to be a long downward spiral of events, was "deregulation", the process through which, broadly, the global telecoms market went through in stages in the 1980s and 1990s, and in the course of which a previously highly regulated market opened itself up to competition. Deregulation, or liberalization as some are wont to call it, remains an ongoing process though it is now far enough advanced that the cat is largely out of the bag and conclusions can be drawn. Both the damage and the positive impact, if that is what they can be called (it varies from geographical location to location), has been done so far as making some sort of judgement is concerned.

DEREGULATION

What is telecoms "deregulation"? In general terms, it is the transition of government authority away from the specific business activities of telephone (and other communications) companies. Deregulation hypothetically seeks to promote new technologies, lower prices, improve services, and to create a more abundant supply of telecoms offerings through opening up markets and introducing competition within them. Broadly, the political landscape in the late 1980s, tilting as it did on the *laissez-faire* competitiveness espoused by the "Reagan–Thatcher" axis, was ripe to see the old, government monopoly infrastructure of telecoms torn down. A liberalized telecoms market would, in many ways, be the ultimate jewel in the Reagan–Thatcher crown provided the course of deregulation ran "right".

It is important to remember that "telecoms" is not (and had never historically been considered) "just another" industry, so telecoms deregulation, viewed from both a commercial and a political perspective, was a truly radical concept. This was particularly true for the notion of global deregulation, since not every country involved in the process would be starting from the same point in terms of the maturity (or sophistication) of its existing domestic network.

Rather, telecoms had always been considered a "backbone" industry that acted as the enabler of commercial, governmental, and social transactions, and as such had (and continues to have) broad geo-political implications. Where the management of, for instance, the retail fashion market might be largely a matter best left to self policing as the sale of clothes has few implications for the national interest, telecoms is a market that lends itself to national strategies and national policies, particularly notable in under-developed countries where teledensity (the percentage of the population with access to the phone network) remains a key developmental issue; hence telecom's regulatory roots.

Prior to deregulation, the telecoms landscape from market-to-market was essentially monopolistic in nature. In short, where there was (in Britain, for instance), once British Telecom alone, the conditions for competition and its attendant benefits were limited or non existent and the likelihood of progressive services lay entirely in the hands of, and at the whim of, the incumbent. Post-deregulation, with BT's competitors now almost a dime a dozen (in mobile as well as fixed services), the market must invariably, at least in theory, be driven forward apace. The result: more opportunity, greater variety, lower prices for the end user.

It is almost impossible to take an entirely dispassionate view of deregulation. At one extreme, one might take a *laissez-faire* approach to the economic arguments in question and support the assertion that a business' right to either explode or implode in a free market should be entirely a matter for the business itself. Competition is good, and any negative consequences are little more than regrettable blips on the profitable march forward. At the other extreme, there is a view that government intervention is positive and necessary to protect the interests of the consumer as well as to promulgate national policy, particularly as business (*sic*) clearly cannot be trusted to police itself, and thus in turn protect the interests of the consumer. Of course, one might argue that a *via media* between the two is a better course than either of the extremes.

What is clear, where telecoms deregulation is concerned, is that in a broad sense with the handing of the keys to a formerly locked asylum to a considerable number of lunatics (the spate of new-born telco players and by knock-on effect, their suppliers amongst them, in the 1990s), it should come as no great surprise that many of these new entities have found it difficult to act with the restraint and judgment necessary to manage the asylum unsupervised and thus to flourish in a competitive market. But on the other hand, some would argue that the problem lies not in the fact, but in the manner in which the keys were handed over, as we shall see.

None of which is to say that deregulation is – or was – a bad thing. It's almost certainly not though some may see it as a necessary evil. However, it does now seem a possibly safe conclusion to state that the course of the deregulatory process (from no competition to such competition as exists today) has not run in a manner as smooth or effective as might have been the case. That the government of the UK, for instance, has now added insult to injury by not only handing over the keys but subsequently levying what amounts to rental charges on their usage (in the form of 3G licenses) smacks at best of poor judgement and at worst sheer greed. On the other hand, there's irony in the fact that a Conservative government spawned such a treasure chest for its Labour successor to subsequently plunder.

THE COST OF LICENSING

In Britain at least, the cost of these license fees has undoubtably been a major contributory factor in the present telecoms recession. As we shall see later, the treasury's rape and pillage of the telecoms market's coffers (above) left little room for manoeuvre once 3G licenses had been acquired. That doesn't excuse a lot of poor decision-making subsequently through which the industry compounded the problem by continuing to shoot itself in the foot, but it does help to illustrate the extent of the feeding frenzy that was the telecoms market in early 2000. Everyone, the Treasury included, wanted their slice of a seemingly limitless pie.

At this point, one can only hope that the hospitals and schools that might be built as a result of these license fees (on the assumption, and increasingly it is an assumption, that they are ever paid in full) will compensate for the damage that has been done to the general economy and in particular the telecoms market itself. It would be naïve in the extreme to believe that the price of failure will be paid by the telecoms titans individually and alone though perhaps when many former CEOs turn to the National Health Service for treatment of their crash-induced nervous breakdowns, they will feel a certain satisfaction in knowing that they are gaining some benefit from the expenditure that lead them to those breakdowns in the first place!

TELECOMS IN THE UK

To return to deregulation, though, what did happen and where and when did things start to go wrong? In Britain, from the early 1980s, measured steps were taken to introduce competition into both the supply of equipment and service provision in the telecoms market. Prior to that time, the General Post Office (established in 1969) had held a monopoly on telecoms in the UK that was broken up as a result of the 1981 Telecommunications Bill (creating a split between the postal and telecoms functions). Initially, the Mercury Consortium received a license that approved the design and build of an independent network that would enable competition with BT across a range of services. Service launch, in 1983, thus saw the battle enjoined, albeit on a limited scale.

In 1984 the British Government (hitherto the sole shareholder in the state monopoly) sold 51 percent of its shares in BT at which time it became a public limited company. Simultaneously the government created Oftel to regulate the newly competitive market (which it did to little effect in the early years of its existence). At this point, the baby wasn't thrown out with the bathwater. Government policy oversaw the creation and management of the BT/Mercury duopoly, in which the number of long distance, fixed line operators was limited to two for a period of seven years. The same sort of "limited" or "managed" competition was attempted in the equipment market. It was not until 1991, when the government sold a further tranche of its holding in BT, that the reins were really loosened.

This process of telecoms deregulation was set to be one of the Thatcher government's defining moments, the transfer of public assets to private ownership being a hallmark of the privatization policies that were a core tenet of what we now know as "Thatcherism." The unforeseen trouble was, and remains, that normal business competition practice does not entirely lend itself to the administration and regulation of former national monopolies and, furthermore, with the duopoly the fundamental nature of the newly deregulated market was false. Thus did the defining moment not exactly become a shining one.

In spite of its commitment to economic liberation, in truth the Conservative government fumbled ahead with a shortage of lucid thinking and a lack of nerve often informing the actual process of deregulation, caught between the rock of wanting to transfer the expense of financing BT's expensive digital future to the private sector, and the hard place of wanting to enrich the treasury in the process. Neither of these factors (commonly known as "having your cake and eating it") was ever likely to result in a truly liberalized market with all the benefits to consumers that would ensue, and the resultant BT/Mercury duopoly thus proved to be something of a sham.

The consequences of this mishandled initial step for the fixed line telecoms market were these. Firstly, a poor example was set for the then embryonic mobile phone market in Britain (which was soon to explode) in which another duopoly was instituted, between BT's mobile arm, Cellnet, and Vodafone. The inevitable result followed: high prices, limited services, and little innovation. Not the result the liberalizers surely had in mind. Secondly, prospective newcomers to both markets were effectively discouraged – if not altogether shut out – at the beginning. The government – encouraged by BT and its undue influence over the regulator – ruled that these newcomers (particularly cable television companies who had a natural pathway for offering telecoms services) should have access to only five million homes each in the first instance. Many argue that these companies strategies were so compromised as a result that they have still not recovered and found a clear sense of direction today. Either way, it was thus not for seven years, until 1993 when OFTEL fell under the leadership of Don Cruikshank, a far more aggressive director general, that a realistic framework for serious liberalization really began to emerge.

What Cruikshank saw was that the real key to encouraging competition lay in the management of interconnection agreements between operators. In a privatized market with many competing service providers, almost any telephone call will, in the course of being "completed", be carried over the physical network of more than one operator. For instance, if you call New York from London, at minimum your call will likely travel over lines owned by, say, BT and AT&T as well as Verizon, which terminates the call. Operators pay each other for transporting portions of calls over their own proprietary lines. As the incumbent and "owner" of the fixed exchanges and national network in the UK, BT was clearly the dominant party in the market and potentially principle beneficiary in any inter- connection policy (as all the competitive operators would invariably have to utilize its network to transport their calls). Cruikshank set about ensuring that the interconnection policy was transparent and, furthermore, attractive to new, competitive telcos.

GLOBAL LIBERALIZATION

The course of telecoms policy in Britain as outlined above is just one example of the emergence of the telecoms market (and its deregulation) as a domestic concern internationally. It makes the point that the issues surrounding liberalization in telecoms were neither straightforward, nor easy. In terms of economic policy, as it has become ever clearer that telecommunications will play a critical role in the modern global economy, so the industry has emerged from being an engine room operation to a subject worthy of national debate and attention. The desire to restructure markets, and thus to speed up the development of services and open them up to the forces of competition led to 69 countries (that control over 80 percent of the world's telecoms traffic between them) signing a binding agreement at the World Trade Organization in Geneva in 1997. This accord committed participants to immediately opening up their domestic markets to foreign competition.

At the time, it was thought that this global liberalization would lead to rich pickings for both operators and equipment manufacturers in established and wealthy markets eager to invest their profits in opportunities further afield, whilst simultaneously benefiting poorer countries keen to attract foreign investment and needing to either build or extend new phone networks or replace existing ones that were near obsolete. As we now know, however, the prospective feeding frenzy of unlimited global opportunity did not work out like that, though it certainly fuelled the spending boom that has now led to bust.

Whilst Britain struggled to overcome the difficulties in the nascent stages of its own open domestic market, the United States pushed hard for the international liberalization of telecoms due in part to the effectiveness (in counterpoint to the British experience) of its own national deregulation policy. The American domestic market had been deregulated quickly and effectively in the 1980s when the former Bell monopoly was broken up into a series of regional operators that became known as the "Baby Bells". These companies prospered quickly (and, unlike their European counterparts, did so largely without saddling themselves with debt) but as they saturated their own markets, they faced the need to expand elsewhere. Before they could do this, global markets needed to be opened up to foreign investment, hence the importance of the WTO accord.

Outside Europe and the United States, the pace of deregulation in the third major region, Asia, proceeded at a slower pace (which did not make the region immune from making the same mistakes made by their western counterparts). Asia was the last zone to fully deregulate its telecoms markets, and competition there has developed more slowly than it did in the US and Europe. As in Europe, history seems to be repeating itself with Asian former incumbents coming under threat in their home markets, struggling to expand abroad, and failing to react effectively to exposure to competition they have no tradition of meeting. Seeking to replace lost domestic revenues and regain some economies of scale, these incumbents too move into overseas markets, usually through a mixture of network expansion and purchase of stakes in overseas operators.

However, they inevitably soon find the network expansion more expensive and more difficult to integrate than they anticipated. Demand for bandwidth also proves to be lower than expected. Their business plans fail to deliver, and poor returns on investments force them to retrench. Meanwhile, they've also taken their eye off the ball at home…

The re-engineered telecoms market that has resulted has thus become truly global in scope. Whether through mergers, acquisitions, or unions between giant telecoms operators (many of whose origins now look increasingly suspect) or through the expansion of supporting players such as equipment providers, it may be argued that the opening up of the global market has provided a greater opportunity for liberalization than that afforded by the more awkward process of opening up domestic markets in many countries. But with internationalization, hot on the heels of liberalization, came a whole new set of problems.

FROM ONE MONOPOLY TO ANOTHER

The concerns include the proposition that old domestic monopolies will ultimately simply be replaced by what are effectively new, multinational ones. Many believe that when all is done and done dusted, the global telecoms market will once again lie in the hands of a few, expansive players who will largely be able to dictate the economic terms within which the market operates. And that is without touching on the arguments pertaining to the social implications of telecoms policy such as whether global deregulation gives the more advanced northern hemisphere countries a further embedded economic advantage over many of their southern counterparts, for instance.

On the other hand, the policy of deregulation has, it can be argued, ultimately met with some success. Across the vast majority of European and developed Asian countries, there have been significant decreases in tariffs since 1998. Hundreds of new operators have been authorized to provide voice telephony services, and there has certainly been improvement in service quality and service diversification as well as a rapid increase in the use of services by consumers. But it is, perhaps, in those statistics as well as in the somewhat troubled and confused nature of the deregulatory process that the seeds of the present problems that the collective market faces lie.

How, then, can deregulation be identified as one of the cars involved in the present pile-up? Is it paradoxical that on the one hand, some markets appear not to have been deregulated quickly and lucidly enough, while on the other the speed of the process of liberalization globally appears to have been equally problematic elsewhere. Is it accidental that the regulatory accord opening up the global market appears to be the point at which, as we shall see later, things really began to spiral out of control in terms of the performance of many companies within the industry itself? Is there such a thing as "too much opportunity?"

There can be little doubt, and the evidence supports the broad assertion, that deregulation broadly brings benefits to the consumer, certainly in the developed world. Even where the road to opening up markets has been confused or over-managed, the end result has been to the advantage of the buyer of telecoms services who now pays, for the most part, less money for a far broader menu of service options. Ironically, however, the victims of ill-conceived policies have tended in some cases to be those companies whose existence as competitors has established the former advantages. In Britain, for example, there is little doubt that Telewest and NTL, the two cable television operators, have both suffered and continue to suffer in a strategic sense from the limitations under which they were originally forced to operate, as we noted earlier.

It can be argued that BT, too, in seeking to protect its monopoly as far as possible either through the management of its relations with the regulator or through dragging its feet in complying with the opening up of its exchanges has shifted its focus from the wider strategic ball and has thus been increasingly incidental as a source of influence in the global telecoms market. Where its equivalents abroad have, in some cases, experienced periods of boom and expansion, BT's global position has waned as it struggled to first comprehend and then to conceive an effective battle plan for the new global marketplace as it sought to protect its position at home.

Global deregulation has also seen the advent of "every man (or company) for himself", with presumed economic self-interest increasingly driving decisions and the quest for profit, compromising the clarity of thinking behind a once more limited telecoms world. The Third World may indeed be right to question whether its national communications interests will be best served by the forces of a market which is driven by distinctions of profitability rather than the need for teledensity, service improvement and innovation, and suchlike. Communications policy (the need, for example, to provide access to poor, rural areas as well as wealthier, urban areas) has always relied on compromise rather than strict economic drivers to point towards desirable outcomes.

FINDING A BALANCE

With the opening up of the global market, players in the telecoms industry, sometimes apparently frenzied by competition, have lost increasing sums of money in these evolutionary markets at least in part due to a failure to identify the right balance between the two. For such companies, the mentality seems often to have been "win the contract at all costs, worry about where the profits will emerge later." It has been a chastening experience for some to learn that winning a contract is not the equivalent of money in the bank. We are reminded of a comment a leading industry figure once made to us about one of his company's rivals, a rival that had spent much of the previous year touting a large number of sales successes, but with little apparently to show for it: he observed "Consistent winners of the world's smallest telecoms contracts. Good luck."

This book, however, is not an attempted analysis of the processes of telecoms deregulation. Deregulation is a stage setter, but not the issue itself. The image that we hope will emerge from this chapter, and it emerges from a most general portrait of the industry over a period of years, is one of uncertainty and confusion, conflicting interests, big visions but an often a more complex reality. It is the story of the difference between the existence of a broad opportunity (the introduction of competition), and knowing what to do with it in specific terms, how to manage it. Far too many in the telecoms industry (whether the subject has been expansion, mergers and acquisitions, product development, entering new markets, or otherwise) have concluded: we will because we can, rather than we can, but how and why?

Deregulation's contribution to the Great Telecoms Swindle is thus, we think, indirect but identifiable. The global management of deregulation, effective in some countries and less so in others but certainly and obviously not uniform may have helped the consumer in a universal sense but, in many, ways, it impeded the market's sense of itself and did not create a level field on which everyone could play. The sheer number of opportunities seems to have worked against the creation of a method for evaluating those opportunities, the emergent logic being (*sic*) that any opportunity must be a good one. A global market might have been created, but one in which each player's hands were tied by the constraints that they still faced. Companies thus exploited their newfound freedom with a great deal of zeal, but in many cases with apparently rather less sense or understanding of the big picture.

Our belief is that the deregulated market that had emerged by the late 1990s, at which point things started to go badly wrong for the telecoms industry at large, was one in which apparent corporate confidence increasingly concealed a myriad of strategic shortcomings. The telecoms world, for so long so relatively placid and structured, had become a highly flammable mixture of opportunity (and egos) tempered by misunderstanding. In effect, the child had been let loose in the candy store, and as events proved he or she was not to show an awful lot of judgement in deciding what to eat. To that extent, deregulation plays its part in the development of the stomach ache that, as we shall see, was to follow.

CASE STUDY

Lucent Technologies

Before deregulation, incumbent network operators largely built and self-developed their own networks, the enabling technology required to effectively manage them, and they also sold telecoms services to a captive audience of consumers. These companies were many-headed beasts. In the course of deregulation, the functions or elements of the traditional telco business were to be broken up and re-launched as independent companies, it now seems much to the industry's disadvantage.

Essentially, whereas there was once the all encompassing "telco" (above), in the course of the 1990s as a result of deregulation, the emergence of competitive carriers, and the booming subsidiary equipment market, a number of businesses came to represent its various parts in the "next generation" world. In very simple terms, service providers were created to provide telecoms services to the end user, but these companies could either have their own networks, or not (in which case they were virtual service providers) as they preferred. Service providers were and essentially are (or should be) experts in the arts of marketing and customer management.

Other companies chose to build and rent capacity on networks, but to have no or little direct contact with the end users of telecoms services. The customers of these companies, like Global Crossing or Carrier 1, were mainly newly formed competitive telcos whose business was bandwidth provision and not network management. Their other customers, as it turned out, were each other.

Some companies, in particular the former incumbents, chose to play or simply played both roles. Some did it effectively, but others were unable to decide where either their futures or their expertise lay and thus, in spite of considerable inherited advantages, a legacy from their monopolistic pasts, floundered when they might and probably should have flourished in the Brave New World.

For all these companies, the network and other equipment necessary to turn vision into telecoms reality was to come from a fourth branch of the new telecoms universe, the equipment provider. Whereas in the past, this function had been an integrated part of the telco, now research and development was an entirely independent function. It stood apart, in corporate terms, from the business it enabled.

What was to become Lucent Technologies was, prior to deregulation in the United States, the network equipment arm of the US giant AT&T, and the jewel in its crown was Bell Labs, a research and development outfit that, it is no exaggeration to say, more or less invented and patented the majority of significant advances in telecommunications over a period stretching almost a century. Lucent, with Bell Labs' repository of Nobel-prize winning scientists, was the privatized business that couldn't go wrong. The company, for a variety of reasons, appeared to have it made.

It really is hard to overestimate the position of strength in which Lucent began its life as an independent company. At least in its primary market its equipment was ubiquitous and, given that telcos are notoriously reluctant to switch suppliers, this meant Lucent was more or less guaranteed a significant future stream of revenues quite apart from the continued servicing of its existing equipment. Furthermore, in a world of network evolution, Bell Labs was the most likely source of future innovation. Even if Lucent didn't play the next-generation game effectively, the circuit switch was not about to become obsolete overnight and in that market, it was king.

Yet, if we fast-forward to today, the unthinkable has happened. In the space of barely a handful of years, Lucent has become a penny stock, threatened with de-listing from the market as its share price has fallen below the $1 threshold for thirty consecutive days. Its annual revenue, once as high as $25 million, has dropped 60 percent in the past two years. Its workforce, which in 1999 numbered more than 150,000 employees, is expected to be no greater than 35,000 within the next twelve months. The only real news surrounding the company today as it announces yet another restructuring is for how much longer can it survive. Not so much if, according to many experts, but when it will give up the ghost. What went wrong?

We have begun to see that the disabled telecoms-market company fits one of two broad genuses. The WorldCom's and Global Crossing's of this world were the brash, upstart newcomers on the block. Lead by pioneering "whiz kids" who ultimately proved visionary only in their ability to line the pockets of themselves and other senior executives, these were the players who quickly flew high and crashed – equally spectacularly – at a comparable velocity.

The Marconi's and the Lucent's of the world lumbered into their distressed present state from the opposite extreme, managed equally incompetently but altogether with neither inspiration or imagination, the lumpen victims in a game which their leadership was never adequately equipped to play. It is no accident that thus far, criminal charges have beset the former without affecting the latter group though that is to be damned by faint praise, to be sure.

Where the WorldComs and Global Crossings arguably never really had even the foundations of success in the short term (though perhaps not in the longer term) but flew high for a while on the back of their collective nous and daring, the Lucent's and Marconi's had all the parts befitting a potentially successful industrial giant (if, in Marconi's case, not in the business of telecoms) but could make absolutely nothing of their heritage, such was the sheer incompetence of the men at the top. What George Simpson was to Marconi, Richard McGinn and his team were to Lucent.

Thus far, the fall of Lucent has not ended up in the bankruptcy courts, though whether the company's road will eventually lead there remains open to question. What is known is that under McGinn the company's strategy of questionable accounting practices, misguided leadership and aggressive lending to customers in a forlorn attempt to meet ambitious revenue targets proved disastrous. The tactics backfired and, at the same time Lucent's customer base (the telcos) entered the crash themselves, seriously compounding the problem. Companies like Winstar Communications, which owed Lucent $700 million, filed for bankruptcy. It is unlikely such debts will ever be paid back.

The markets reactions to Lucent's troubles has been swift. Its shares have dropped from the region of $67 to, today, around 75¢. The company is now considering a reverse split to maintain its position on the New York Stock Exchange.

In addition to the collapse of its customer base to whom, when times were good, the company had almost wrecklessly lent money to fund the purchase of its equipment, Lucent's deep pockets had enabled it to make a string of acquisitions in the late 1990s. Snatching up "hot" companies, often innovative smaller players whose expertise, generally, lay in the next-generation segment of the market in which Lucent was not traditionally dominant (and where Cisco Systems threatened, if it had not already, to usurp Lucent's position as the dominant telco network equipment provider as the network migrated to an IP backbone), it proved beyond Lucent's management to either formulate a clear forward strategy or, indeed, to run their acquisitions effectively as part of the expanded company. Thus, acquisitions large and small were made apparently willy-nilly, including the likes of Agere Systems which has now been spun off and cutting-edge software provider Kenan, sold on for a fraction of what Lucent paid for it. Lucent, it seemed, expanded because it seemed like a good idea at the time without ever having much idea how to proceed once the cheque had been written.

Part of the problem was the Lucent mindset. With the entrenched mentality of a former incumbent, Lucent brought a Dickensian business style to an increasingly innovative age. Where the new breed of infrastructure provider was lithe, reactive, and innovative – focused on the direction in which telecoms was heading, Lucent was sticky toffee pudding in an age in which sushi was the diet of choice. The company offered no clear vision, no real roadmap, little sense of purpose, and an absence of energy or vitality. When it imported such talent, it often departed unsatisfied. Lucent was almost an anomaly within the market they once dominated. The companies it acquired with the presumably secondary intention (after revenue) of dragging it into the future were, in fact, dragged down themselves once a part of the Lucent milieu.

Nonetheless, for a time Lucent's revenue soared as the flood of fledgling post-deregulation telcos placed orders for its equipment. After that market collapsed, even Lucent's traditional core customers (the major local and long distance phone companies) would keep its head above water for a while until they, too started (often for the first time in their histories) to reduce spending levels. When that happened, Lucent was quickly in serious trouble. It had underwritten purchases (effectively gaining revenue) which were never going to be paid. The company's temporary success had been the result of a false economy. Its poor management and ineffective acquisitions added insult to injury.

In some ways, no downfall has been quite so spectacular as that of Lucent. This, via Bell Labs, was the company largely responsible for the history of modern telecoms technology, including the invention of the transistor and the laser, and the creation of the Unix operating system. To run such a legacy to within inches of its life, and Lucent's future now is very far from assured, takes directorial incompetence of an exceptional and rarely seen scale.

CHAPTER 4

Hard cell

The telecoms world goes mobile

If liberalization in fixed telecoms markets is, for the general reader, important to understand in the context of this book but nonetheless largely an abstraction in broader terms and the slow demise of the circuit switched fixed network plus the attendant onset of next generation networks and services is, though slightly more familiar territory still largely specific to those in the world of telecoms, the mobile explosion that occurred during the 1980s and 1990s is somewhat different.

The explosion of mobile telephony, perhaps more than any of the other changes that have in recent years revolutionized the telecoms market is the part of the puzzle that we have all held in the palm of our hands. In a way, "vanilla" (as it's known) mobile is what 3G hasn't become . . . the telecoms boom that delivered on its promise. Where, in the early and mid 1980s, more or less none of us were users of mobile telephony, little more than a decade later in most of the world's developed markets, the mobile handset was ubiquitous.

The reason for this is simple, and we will return to it elsewhere: unlike almost any other change or advance in the telecoms market in the period in question, the world was decidedly ready for mass-market mobile; it was only the development of technology which had held it back. With familiarity with the service offered established at the outset (which, more or less, simply enhanced the voice telecoms service that we all used already by making it portable), mobile couldn't fail. It thus did not "change" telecoms from the perspective of the consumer. It simply made it "better".

Given this positive state of affairs, why can at least a few of the seeds of doom in relation to the crash be traced to the rapid and positive experiences of the evolution of mobile telecoms?

THE ORIGINS OF MOBILE TELEPHONY

To start with a history, mobile telephony was not born overnight. In fact, the "roots" of mobile date back to the United States in the 1920s, when a number of police departments across North America sought to deploy the same technology that was used in ocean liners to improve safety in patrol cars. This service was known as "radiotelephone". The plan, however, didn't materialize. The technology, which could be reasonably housed on ships, was far too awkward and outsized to be used in cars, apart from which the uneven geography of land (as opposed to the flat sea) made the transmission of signals nigh on impossible.

The enabling technological breakthrough that made land-based mobile technically feasible was FM (frequency modulation), which arrived in 1935 courtesy of Edwin Howard Armstrong. Designed for radio broadcasting, FM reduced the sheer size of radio equipment whilst simultaneously improving signal quality. This development played a vital part in

World War 2, where higher quality, two-way communications were needed in battle. The performance and potential in military scenarios didn't escape the notice of leading companies such as AT&T, Motorola, and General Electric back in the States. A number of products that had their roots in the war (such as walkie-talkies) were adapted from war time technology and came to play a role in civilian life afterwards.

The first true mobile telephone services date back to the 1940s, though with limited capacity and few available radio channels they were hardly widely available to the public. AT&T, in 1947 however, increased the number of radio frequencies available to mobile by placing a number of low-power transmitters across a metropolitan area that effectively passed calls between themselves as phone users moved around. This technique allowed more users to access the system by not tying up limited frequencies and represents, to all intents and purposes, the real "birth of mobile."

If the idea, from a technological perspective worked, the service was still years ahead of its time (perhaps offering a parallel for the present day 3G mess, though that will be of scant consolation to the industry). It was another 20 years before the technology had been refined to the point where mass market mobile communications could even be considered, after which the Federal Communications Commission still had to approve the principle of cellular service before it could proceed unabated.

Thus, by the early 1970s the stage was set and in 1973 Motorola launched its DynaTAC phone, a "reasonably" sized mobile. In 1977 the FCC awarded two experimental licenses, one in Chicago (to AT&T) and one in Washington (to Motorola and American Radio Telephone Service), at which time it began to consider the issue of licensing commercial mobile service.

In May 1981, two licenses were announced for each leading US market, to be awarded first to a "new entrant" (a non fixed line carrier) and second to the local fixed phone company. These would cover 75 percent of the urban population and 25 percent of the rural population, whilst covering 80 percent of the US landmass. Within a short time of announcing the licenses, the FCC was mired in applications. Hundreds of them poured in and the "comparative hearings" through which they would be judged thus proved unfeasible. It cost more than a million dollars to award one license alone.

At this point, in 1983, the FCC announced a new lottery system as literally thousands of applications continued to mount up. By 1984, Washington DC did have two competing wireless providers but it was almost a decade later before the necessary construction permits had been granted to enable systems in all the markets originally identified to get up and running. The subscriber count topped five million by the end of 1990, and passed ten million approximately two years later.

In August 1993, President Clinton's Omnibus Budget Reconciliation Act authorized the FCC to auction Personal Communications Services, a group of cellular radio services designed for individual and business use. It was thought this would open the door to advanced services such as paging and data. One hundred and two PCS licenses were awarded, in fifty-one areas. Billions of dollars were raised by the auctions, leading to the creation of significantly more licenses. The market, originally built on the supposition of two carriers per area supported, by 1995, nine. US mobile had taken off though, as it turned out, somewhat less explosively than was the case elsewhere.

THE EUROPEAN STORY

In Europe, the birth of mobile did not follow the same path as it had across the Atlantic. During the early 1980s, the largely impractical analogue systems took some hold and the market experienced fairly rapid growth, especially in Scandinavia and the UK and to a lesser extent elsewhere in Northern Europe. The analogue systems deployed were, however, unique to each country's market and lacking technical standardization. This meant that the equipment and operational functionality of each separate network lacked the ability to interface with others.

The result of this reality was to place a massive constraint on the exploitation of the potential of the mobile market which, effectively, was limited by national boundaries at a minimum. Particularly in the context of an increasingly unified political Europe at the time, the status quo made little sense. Not only was the primary market (for mobile communications) fenced in in terms of potential expansion but, furthermore, as equipment and economies of scale were limited for the same reason, the secondary market was also certain to fail to maximize its opportunities. Small, local telcos and specific equipment manufacturers with limited markets were the order of the day.

In Europe, at least, the scale of the problem was taken on board early on and in 1982 the Conference of European Posts and Telegraphs formed a study group called Groupe Speciale Mobile which set about grasping the nettle of investigating the development of a Europe-wide mobile telephony system. A number of criteria were identified which such a system would have to meet and in turn the meeting of which would likely result in a subsequent mobile explosion. These included voice quality, low terminal and service cost, support for international roaming, ISDN compatibility and more.

In 1989, their work was turned over to the European Telecommunications Standards Institute (ETSI) who, within a year, had published phase one of the specifications envisioned for the new network. Commercial GSM service was launched in mid-1991 and within as little as two years, there were over thirty GSM networks in twenty-two countries across Europe with another twenty-five actively considering joining them.

The GSM standard, furthermore, was not Europe-only. South Africa, Australia, and much of the orient also selected it so that from a small, limited series of intra-national mobile markets in 1991, scarcely over two years later GSM (which now stands for Global System for Mobile Telecommunications) had transformed mobile telecoms into an international market with over 1.3 million subscribers globally.

This "birth of mobile" revolutionized the telecoms market from a far greater perspective than simply altering the life of the consumer by putting new technology in his or her hand. Just as the traditional, fixed-line market had its infrastructure (hardware and software) so a multi-billion dollar equivalent market for the mobile world sprang into life almost overnight. It may be dramatic to employ such phrasing, but it is not far from the truth.

Mobile network operators needed mobile networks and their attendant elements (base stations, switches, etc.), operational support systems, and business support systems, the great majority of which needed to be designed to cater specifically to the technological requirements of mobile. Systems (for billing, for example) that had long worked in the fixed network world were not necessarily adaptable to mobile. Existing telecoms suppliers developed mobile product lines to meet this demand, and moreover new companies were born catering specifically for the nascent mobile market (many of whom eventually made the jump in the other direction, and came to develop products for the fixed line market too in spite of their initial insistence that the future lay solely in mobile).

As such, new giants were born, and old fixed line giants came to face serious indirect and sometimes direct competition, in many ways for the first time at least in terms of the depth and intensity of the competition itself. Throughout the 1990s such a wealth of opportunities generally abounded that few took the time to consider the long-term picture though, inevitably, the well had at some point to run dry.

NEW PLAYERS EMERGE

This state of affairs resulted in the creation of a market apparently packed with prospective financial gain, little of which was truly understood. If we pause momentarily for reflection, we can see, in the late 1990s, that if we can move beyond the notion of telecommunications as simply being the "traditional fixed line phone business", the market was actually in many ways an almost completely new and highly immature one. Many of the increasingly influential players within it (either suppliers or telcos) were latecomers in historical terms, and they bought with them neither a developed understanding of their industry nor cultures that fit in with many of the market's traditions. These were lithe, new companies in a world traditionally dominated by bloated monopolies.

This was, in many ways, no bad thing. The cutting edge, visionary business "style" and marketing acumen of the newcomers brought to the telecoms world by the likes of Orange and their ilk was much needed. The former fixed-world incumbents (BT, Deutsche Telekom, etc.) were effectively dinosaurs that desperately needed to be shaken out of their complacent approach, and the mobile explosion thus resulted in a breath of fresh air blowing through the entire telecoms sector.

Still, the divergent styles, "old" way and "new" way, meant that within that market inevitable complications would arise. The obvious example is the mergers and acquisitions between traditional and next generation companies who, it turned out, barely understood each other let alone had the ability to work effectively together. Lucent's woeful failure to grasp and absorb these realities contributed much to its subsequent downfall as it bought "next generation" suppliers for billions and, in a matter of months, is now selling them off for pennies (when they can sell them off at all). Many of the former incumbents also embarked on acquisition sprees characterized more by the intent to "keep up" than by any clear understanding of what they were keeping up with. In the absence of having a well conceived business strategy, buying someone . . . anyone . . . appeared to be acceptable as long as you weren't standing still. Or at least that's how it often seemed at the time.

The fixed line market had been turned upside down by deregulation (the course of which had run smoothly in some geographies and far less effectively in others), the mobile market had more or less been invented (at least as a mass market) overnight and as we'll learn in subsequent chapters the network itself was on the point of revolution too, about to undergo a dramatic change in what we perceive telecoms services to be. Due to the opportunities afforded by deregulation and the sheer size of the mobile market opportunity money was flowing into telecommunications, but largely on the basis of predicting the future of an industry that, in its present state, had very little past with which to provide a guide for likely outcomes in the years ahead.

ORGANIZED CHAOS

The reality, in many ways, was something akin to organized chaos. As, in the course of the 1990s, the tap of opportunity remained on so reputations were made and the die was to some extent cast. The politics of personality came to be as prevalent as the controls of the balance sheet in decision-making, and the likes of Hans Snook (Orange), Chris Gent (Vodafone), Bernie Ebbers (WorldCom) and their ilk became the recognisable face of the telecoms industry (which is not to tar all with the same brush in the end). Protestations like the "fixed line telecoms has no future" became taken as "statements of fact", and the CEOs (in other industries, too) saw themselves increasingly taking on the mantle of public celebrity, like professional athletes or actors . . . expected to have, and acting as if they had, "star quality". Ego in many cases ran rampant, and the financial markets gave it reason to do so as the WorldCom story itself now belatedly reveals. Many of the leading companies seemed to suggest they could grow significantly year-on-year, almost ad infinitum. And no one really questioned (until it was too late) the likely reality behind such a notion.

In the mobile world, after the initial explosion of birth, the problems inevitably set in. Operators subsidizing handsets to sign up customers, then losing them to competitor's cheaper tariffs before having recouped the acquisition expense originally involved. This subscriber "churn", almost a dirty word within the industry, even in the early days betrayed the fact that the course of opportunity wasn't running smoothly. It was almost impossible to know how well a mobile operator was performing because the customer numbers presented were always a fudge. Anything except real, active subscriber counts would be offered to present a best face for the world. For the customer, liberalization and the birth of mobile may have been all good on the face it, but choice alone doesn't guarantee a healthy financial future for those behind the service.

KNOWING YOUR CUSTOMER – OR NOT

In fact, the reality was that telcos were coming to know almost everything except that which lay at the heart of their businesses – namely customers – and therein lay a sizeable problem. In a highly competitive market the key to success invariably lies in understanding your buyer and developing a relationship with him or her. Telcos had access to mountains of information (usage data, demographics, payment patterns) about their customers, all keys to effectively developing services and schemes for customer retention and, ultimately, increasing profitability. But half the time they weren't accessing that information and the other half it was being used ineffectively if at all. The battleground was set as "how many customers have we got or how many can we get?" rather than "how can we profit from them?". Sheer weight of numbers does not necessarily translate to a corresponding increase in revenue.

This reality gave birth to another sub-industry and another telecoms-related boom market; for customer relationship management (CRM) solutions, a concept perhaps yet to be revealed as just more hype and doggerel. Certainly we remember dining with a leading industry executive back in 1999 who, off the record, asked us: "What the hell are people thinking? If you haven't been doing customer service for years, do you really think CRM is going to come in and change things now?"

CRM sounded like a nice idea, but like so many aspects of progress it was one to which lip service was paid through investment in systems which, all too often, were barely "turned on". From a strictly personal perspective, just in the past few weeks we have been told by our phone company that it lacks the capability to change the date of the direct debit via which we pay our monthly bill, and by our mobile service provider that it cannot tell us the state of our account up to today's date. This is the brave new world of real time billing and enhanced relationships with the customer?

On the other hand, the finance industry had provided something of a lead to the telecoms market. Having coped with deregulation itself and learned to manage the customer relationship far more effectively in the process, it gave the telecoms industry something of a road map with which to face oncoming challenges many of which were not dissimiliar to those the telecoms industry now faced in the wake of deregulation and increased competition. Unfortunately, the telecoms mindset often prevailed. The focus of carriers tended for the most part to be on network building and, in the burgeoning mobile market, on sheer marketing. The meat in the sandwich went missing. Few really wanted to invest in somewhat costly systems that might help to run a business effectively, if they could invest in systems that might grow it. Scale, as an end unto itself, consistently prevailed over stability. CRM, even today, is talked about more for its potential than its actual application.

The conclusion is that the mobile explosion didn't inherently harm the telecoms market, but rather that the emergent market harmed itself (*sic*). The crisis was a crisis of leadership and vision (or the lack of it). The mobile opportunity was fundamentally good, the management of it was often woeful. What's happening now (consolidation, and the progressive development of networks and services slowing down at a remarkable rate if not grinding to a halt altogether) attests to that fact. 3G became the straw that broke the camel's back, but if it hadn't been 3G it would have been something else. The corporate history of the mobile telecoms explosion is truly a tale conceived by idiots, initially full of loud and furious expenditure, signifying little more than enormous fiscal loss . . . for the time being at any rate. That may, almost certainly will, slowly change in the future as the real winners emerge, but not before pause has been given to right the listing ship first and the Great Telecoms Swindle has been overcome.

MANAGEMENT IGNORANCE

What were the chief executives of the mobile telecoms world thinking in those days? Did each and every one believe that they had simply entered into a race for scale that the investment world was willing to finance and if they just ran the race then they could not lose? Never mind that in so doing, their actions would simply serve to drive up the price of every merger and every acquisition into which they entered, thus driving another nail into their own coffins in the process. Was that (effectively spend, spend, spend mentality) considered a viable business model?

For many, the answer is apparently yes. But a race can only have so many winners. And thus it has come to pass that it's commonly accepted that whilst those few players with real (global) scale will survive the present hardships of the depressed market, many are going to the wall simply because their initial tactics were so woefully wrong. It seems never to have occurred to some that opportunity is finite . . . that it was just possible that too much bandwidth or a limited potential customer base might impact their futures in a negative way.

The depth of ignorance underlying the assumptions on which so many decisions were made is staggering.

It can also be argued that the mobile telecoms world ignored managing its dusty corridors correctly, or at all, in the endless quest to play itself out in the glamorous world of international finance. It often overlooked or failed to invest in the back-room systems that would have enabled it to function more effectively . . . and in so doing it betrayed the very people that might have kept it afloat . . . its customers. Mobile telcos spent billions on licenses for the next generation of services, yet were reluctant to spend thousands or a few million on systems to manage those present already. It assumed the people wanted what it wanted to give them, rather than giving them what they needed in the first place. And, as failure became more and more inevitable, the options for survival became more limited. The manner in which the game, for many, ended, has revealed just what those options were. Few of them make for pleasant reading now.

Nonetheless, if the mobile explosion lies prominently in the background to the Great Telecoms Swindle, one element of the mobile story still remains outstanding in identifying the causes of the crash, and it is to the subject of 3G that we will now turn our attention.

CASE STUDY

WorldCom

We left WorldCom at the end of the first chapter of this book bankrupt and facing a welter of Congressional and court investigations. In the ensuing months, though the entire story has yet to come to light, the scale of the company's fall and the misjudgements made, to put it charitably, continues to be revealed.

On August 22nd Salomon Brothers, the investment banking firm, released documents that revealed that it had allocated more than 100,000 shares in Initial Public Offerings to senior officers and directors of WorldCom. In a period between January 1996 and November 1997, the brokerage firm had enabled a number of WorldCom leaders to make an average profit of $2.3 million each through shares received at the offer price which were then sold when prices rose after the markets had opened for trading.

Salomon Brothers provided neither the names nor the precise number of WorldCom executives who had received these share allocations, nor did they name the firms whose shares were involved. Confidentiality policies, apparently (not to mention conveniently), prevented the release of this information. The documents had been released as a result of a subpoena from the Congressional committee investigating the role of Jack Grubman. Essentially, the charge was that the shares had been directed to WorldCom leaders in return for lucrative investment banking business for Salomon. Grubman, amazingly, had been unable to recall whether IPO allocations had been given to WorldCom in his own, earlier, testimony.

In its own defence (how the rich get richer), Salomon says that its actions amounted to common practice and were entirely consistent with industry regulations. It was, apparently, quite normal for hot IPO shares to be distributed to major clients. That might have been true – at the time, the investigating committee declined to comment – but it was becoming clear that on such regulations was built the landscape on which an entire market could impale itself built. Legal or not, something smelled very rotten indeed.

Two weeks later, WorldCom chief executive John Sidgmore agreed to leave his post with creditors expressing concern that the company needed entirely fresh management to navigate a course through the catastrophe. Even his own board were divided. He would continue to hold his position while a successor was found, then revert to his role of vice-chairman.

The announcement was made at a board meeting during which a court-appointed monitor had raised the issue of loans to Bernie Ebbers, and a contract with another board member, Stiles A. Kellett, Jr, to lease a corporate jet from WorldCom for the princely sum of $1 a month, a benefit presumably not widely available to all employees. Given that Kellet was a member of WorldCom's compensation committee, responsible for approving the loans to Ebbers, a conflict of interest was noted.

Kellet, for his part, denied any wrongdoing and defended the agreement, noting that he himself had (generously, we think) paid for maintenance, fuel, and crew for the jet, in addition to which he paid a sum to WorldCom for each hour the plane was in flight. Denuded shareholders will no doubt feel palliated by such a display of largesse.

For that selfless explanation, Kellet was asked to respond formally to questions about the lease the following month. At the same time, the monitor told the WorldCom board that there may be grounds to cancel Ebbers' own severance agreement with the company, though the board decided to take no action itself.

Sidgmore was criticized by the monitor for high priced contracts with investment banks and consultants that he had entered into in the course of the company's demise. These – worth millions of dollars – were signed without board approval, though Sidgmore claimed he needed advice as he sought to dispose of WorldCom assets in the course of the ongoing bankruptcy. So much for the job of repairing the company's tainted image with the public and Wall Street.

By late September, the first green bottle fell from the WorldCom wall. David F. Myers, the company's former controller, pleaded guilty to charges that he had manipulated accounting in order to inflate profits and that, furthermore, he had then tried to cover up his actions. Federal prosecutors now had the bit firmly between their teeth. Myers told a judge in US District Court that, furthermore, he was directed by his superiors to do what he had done. Predictably, his plea was part of a deal arranged to help the government nail down the men at the top of the WorldCom swindle.

Myers pleaded guilty to three counts of conspiracy, securities fraud, and making false statements to the SEC who, in response, filed their own civil complaint against him. He faces a multi-million dollar fine and up to twenty years in prison though because of his co-operation, that will likely be reduced. His actions were taken to ensure that WorldCom's accounts met analyst's expectations.

In court, Myers described a group of WorldCom employees who were involved in what he had done, but failed to name names. He said: "I was instructed on a quarterly basis by senior management to ensure that entries were made to falsify WorldCom's books to reduce WorldCom's actual reported costs and therefore to increase WorldCom's reported earnings."

He added, "Along with others who worked under my supervision, and at the direction of WorldCom senior management, such accounting adjustments were made for which I knew there was no justification or documentation and were not in accordance with generally accepted accounting principles."

Unsurprisingly, WorldCom chose not to comment on Myers' plea. Investigators were hopeful that, at a minimum, enough evidence would emerge to indict Scott Sullivan who was described in court documents as the ringleader of attempts to defraud the company's investors.

As we write, Buford Yates, Jr, WorldCom's former accounting director, has joined Myers by pleading guilty to his part in the accounting fraud. His plea came in response to two charges of securities fraud and conspiracy, for which he faces a term of fifteen years in prison. It was revealed that Yates had been helping the government for two months. At least two of Yates' employees were expected to swell the number of guilty pleas and further assist the prosecutor's case.

The significance of Yates' plea appears to be that the net is closing in on Ebbers. As pending convictions move up the food chain, the pressure will now turn to Sullivan as the investigation nears the very top. Yates, for his part, claimed that he did express his reservations to superiors about the actions he had taken, but was overruled. He would not speculate on whether Ebbers was aware of what had been going on.

Scott Sullivan's team had now largely turned. Four of the direct employees of the former WorldCom chief financial officer are today working on the government's side and the case that Sullivan masterminded the fraud apparently gathers steam. It is only a short leap from where we now stand to the top of mountain itself. Both Sullivan and Ebbers lie quiet for the present.

Was it WorldCom or is it WorldCon? The answer to that question, without prejudging what remains to emerge and the judgement of the courts, seems fairly clear. But what does that tell us about the nature of the Great Telecoms Swindle? We must speculate on circumstance and motivation as well as action in order to reach a judgement. We shall attempt to do that in the remaining pages of this book.

CHAPTER 5

A license to thrill?

The roller-coaster world of 3G services

No acronym quite so thoroughly encapsulates and defines an industry as comprehensively as "3G" does the telecoms market at the present time. Think telecoms, and 3G is what almost certainly comes to your mind. It is the metaphorical racehorse on which countless players in the world of mobile telecommunications have put almost all of their cash, and it is the vision with which many of them have chosen to build their future relationship with their customers. In short, the fate of the market hinges, as we are now seeing, largely on the fate of 3G. It is the self-proclaimed Great White Hope of the telecommunications industry.

3G is thus the technology upon which many supposedly shrewd and successful decision-makers have banked their future. It has become the service that will either deliver vastly greater profits or, conversely, it will bring the market down altogether. To date, it is doing the latter. Marconi, whose story we will look at in greater detail later, is indirectly a prime example and a salutary tale of what can happen when a new world order (if not 3G specifically) is bought hook, line and sinker.

We need to begin by defining what, first of all, is meant by the phrase 3G. In literal terms, 3G describes third generation mobile telecoms services, which is to say those services that are the successors to the original analogue and then limited digital services with which we as consumers have been familiar to date, and which were known sequentially as second and 2.5 generation, discussed in an earlier chapter.

Where the simple transition from basic analogue (1G) to GSM (2G) networks drove the first mobile explosion, it has always been the complex and diverse range of third, or "next" generation services that would, it was promised, open the door both to the true potential of mobile telecoms technology to revolutionize our lives and, in turn, to untold profits for the service provider and equipment manufacturer alike. 3G thus evolved into something (almost an "entity" in itself) that has taken on messianic proportions. Unfortunately, the tale of its unfolding bears a remarkable similiarity to the story of the emperor's new clothes.

To put an explanation of 3G in the hands of one of its apostles, we quote from Nokia's website:

> First there was voice. Then there was text messaging. Now, we are on the brink of mobile communications as varied and powerful as our imaginations.
>
> With 3G mobile communication standards and technologies we will communicate using voice, text, images and video:
>
> - 3G is being on a train and watching clips from your favourite soap

- 3G is being out and sending images back to headquarters
- 3G is using your phone to take holiday pictures to instantly send to your friends back home
- 3G is using your phone for a videoconference in a taxi.

And so on, ad infinitum. Ad nauseam. This is the promise or vision that has been hammered first into the industry itself, and then into the consumer market with a fervour bordering on zealous in recent years.

WHO WANTS "3G"?

The most obvious problem along the way has been that someone apparently forgot to ask the person who would make these services profitable – the consumer at whom this brave new world is aimed — whether he or she actually wanted any of the glittering advances mentioned above? And even more importantly what, if any additional sum of money, they'd be willing to pay for them? There is a story we tell that relates to an interview with someone we can reasonably describe as an industry visionary and whose company was built largely on the backbone of providing a unique enabling component of the 3G food chain. Having long argued the merits of services such as those above (and having made millions on the strengths of his arguments), we put it to this gentleman that if 3G did take off, pornography would inevitably be a highly lucrative and popular service (for evidence, see the development of cable television and World Wide Web content offerings).

There's nothing like the suggestion of a little immorality to bring out the puritan in any industrial market executive and we were quickly rebuffed with the apocryphal response: "Pornography won't work on 3G because the pictures will be too small (*sic*)." And there, in a nutshell, the telecoms industrys own logic is laid bare. Answers are tailored for the individual question . . . the screen too small to make m-pornography viable will, nevertheless, be large enough to support a clip from your favourite soap opera. Size, it appears, may matter but only on an entirely *ad hoc* basis. Let us assure that if and when 3G reaches critical mass, pornography will be in the vanguard if there's so much as a sniff of profit in the air.

That the industry was struggling for comprehensive, or even credible answers to key 3G questions should have been obvious from the start. Right now, the banks holding all those 3G-related notes are going to take a profit wherever and however they can get it.

But that is to get ahead of ourselves.

So, again, what else is 3G? Third generation mobile is a technology that will see the creation of a "pipe" for providing mobile access to Internet-based services. The pipe is the medium through which content is transmitted. In the original world of fixed line telecoms, the physical "pipe" was formed by copper wires in the ground, an inflexible medium not good for much more than the transmission of voice. The new pipe (highly flexible with regard to potential content) is 3G's underlying great leap forward.

In short, from the end user's perspective, 3G means the mobile phone handset will be able to do an awful lot more than transmit the familiar voice and, latterly, text messaging services with which we are now familiar and, in turn, it means the mobile phone will have the potential to play an extended role in our lives. If we want it to . . . this is key.

To give you some idea of how extreme the technological great leap forward to 3G is, to download a three-minute MP3 song using 2G technology takes around half an hour and possibly a little more (through what can be called today's thin pipe). To download the same song over a 3G backbone would take less than a minute (the new, advanced pipe being "fat").

KEY BENEFITS

There are some clear-cut advantages to the new 3G world that are advances beyond argument. For one, 3G systems have a high commonality of design on a worldwide basis, with an equal compatibility of services and handsets that share global roaming capability, something that was demonstrably not the case with earlier mobile standards. On a purely technical level, 3G *is* an advance. What 3G does in very simple terms is to allow the telco to improve and expand the services that it is able to offer the end user or customer. It is important to make this distinction, therefore, when evaluating 3G. Is it the specific technology that is in trouble now, or is it what it may be used for: the future of the services themselves?

The key to 3G is, clearly, data (as opposed to voice) services in part for the simple reason that existing methodologies already provide adequate support for traditional services. If voice were to continue to be more or less the sole backbone of telecoms (in which case, where would expanded profits come from?), then 3G might be desirable but not so desirable as to demand the investment that it has generated. 3G, in other words, really only works if the new services take off. Therein lies the reward for the investment.

As we now know, current GSM networks are not optimized for data transmission and whilst the abilities of those networks were enhanced by add-on technologies like GPRS and EDGE which enabled varying degrees of mobile Internet access, the industry would argue that these satisfied only the initial requirement for mobile data services, with neither going the whole nine yards and thus neither being viable as a long-term option. The presumption, however, lies in the desirability of the enhancements 3G can provide.

The major 3G system under development is UMTS, the acronym standing for "Universal Mobile Telecommunications System". This has been developed within a framework defined by the ITU known as IMT-2000. Projections suggest that UMTS will support a mass market for 3G services that will exceed over 2 billion users worldwide by the year 2010, and be worth over one trillion US dollars to mobile operators over the next ten years (which, being facetious, provokes the question about why so many of them are now going out of business, which lies in fact at the heart of this book).

The point is, and the key word above is, "projections". The "build it and they will come" assumption underlying the birth of 3G has been rapidly exposed as faulty thinking of the highest order. In the first instance, this may be due to misinterpretations of the reasons behind the initial success of mobile telecoms.

WHY GSM SUCCEEDED (AND WHY 3G MIGHT FAIL)

GSM worked. The explosion of mobile services globally in the last fifteen to twenty years, not to mention the balance sheets of leading service providers, attest conclusively to that fact. The question, a particularly problematic one in light of the trials and tribulations of 3G, is why? Many industry analysts (who, like all analysts, have something of a vested interest in the conclusions they reach) were inclined to believe that GSM proved the universal popularity of mobile communications. Period. In reality, this conclusion now appears to be seriously erroneous.

When GSM networks first took root, there can be little doubt that there was enormous pent-up demand for mobile telephony. Old style analogue mobile systems (pre the mid 1980s) were of neither sufficient quality nor scale to render the mass marketing of handset devices possible and these handsets were, in any case, not the slimline and user friendly devices of today. Thus, historically, mobile penetration until the mid-to-late-1980s was very low. Few countries in Europe, for instance, even had competing networks (the UK was an exception). The advent of GSM fundamentally changed the equation, and created the market in the form with which we are familiar today; cheap handsets, open competition, high penetration of services among the population, and extensive international coverage. What the heralds of 3G overlooked was the pre-existing conditions in the market that made the success of

GSM almost inevitable did not exist for the introduction of 3G. Many people are quite happy with the mobile service they presently receive and don't want "more" (i.e. mobile data). If "more" does sound appealing, even then it is probably not so appealing that people will necessarily pay for it. Few are dissatisfied with current service provision, handsets, and the like; conversely, dissatisfaction with analogue was high. The arena is altogether different.

In short there's a difference, even for a prospectively "desirable" service, in going from something to nothing versus expanding an already successful base. To use an analogy, at the birth of the mass automotive market early in the last century, the likely popularity of cars was probably assured some time before they became widely affordable and available because transport is a requirement and the mode of independent transport that cars represented was entirely new. Thus, when cars became available to the masses, a vastly successful and profitable market was established.

However, once established, it no longer follows that the development of bigger or better or faster cars (no matter how revolutionary the advances) will result in a revolution in the market as explosive as that which occurred at the market's birth. The simple fact is that Ferrari may make, by an arbitrary standard, the "best" cars in the world today, but not everyone drives one, not everyone wants to pay for one (even among those people who can afford a Ferrari) and, most importantly of all, not everyone covets one. Furthermore, when a breakthrough in automotive technology is established, it does not follow that consumer purchasing patterns of cars will change overnight. Semi-automatic gear shifts may have dominated the top end of Formula One recently and are no doubt the technology of the future. Nevertheless, they appear on a limited number of road cars and there is no apparently rush amongst consumers to purchase those that do presently have the technology.

In short, one failure of the telecoms market (amongst analysts and participants alike) has been to seriously over-egg the 3G pudding, to assume that just as GSM heralded a revolution so, with 3G, history must inevitably repeat itself and another paradigm shift occur. It won't. The underlying market conditions that gave birth to the initial revolution no longer exist. That, surely, is now beyond debate. GSM had a second inherent advantage over 3G, and that was its ease of use. Consumers did not need to acquire, or need to be sold an application nor did they need to learn how to use the service. With 2G, all you needed to do was talk as you'd do on the fixed telephone systems with which consumers were already familiar.

Nonetheless, late in the 1990s it became clear that 3G was, as we said at the start of this chapter, the horse that those involved in the telecoms market were collectively going to back to carry it into a brave (and profitable) new communications world. In making such an epochal decision, the industry was presenting itself with a series of enormous opportunities and, simultaneously, a series of potentially equally enormous problems (or at best challenges) the handling of which would inevitably be make or break for many of those involved. One key question now appears to be whether anybody appreciated the scale of the undertaking that the birth of 3G represented:

most knew where they wanted to go but many apparently knew neither how to get there nor what they'd do once they arrived. As a result, the blind in many cases ended up leading the blind.

THE ALL-NEW CHALLENGE

What must be appreciated is that 3G, as it was advertised from the perspective of the telecoms market, represents revolution, not evolution. This point has been argued in detail by those involved in the industry who, first, sided with the former notion and latterly, when it became clear that the road ahead would not be a straightforward one, have tended towards the latter. If what you're doing isn't working, why claim to be a revolutionary after all? 3G was, however, never a technology that could be instituted by building on existing infrastructure, that could be brought about by modifying devices already in use, or (as we have seen) that would succeed simply by enhancing an existing service offering. 3G was and continues to be a ground-up challenge. It is fundamentally different which is why we are still awaiting its arrival today.

To give some idea of the scale of this challenge, we can look at the basic nature of the traditional telco and, by extension, its suppliers and customers. In the old telecoms world, as we know, voice was key. Phone companies made their money from transporting voice calls over long-proven "wires in the ground" networks, and the end user (customer) paid for usage on these networks on the basis of time and distance (how far each call travelled, how long it lasted). You'd pay more for a twenty minute call from London to New York than you would for a one minute call to a local destination. In short, telecoms was based on a reasonably simple economic model and the infrastructure required to support this model was long established. The systems (for network management) and the elements of the network itself needed to make the model work (such as the technology required to produce a phone bill) were in place. The model was profitable, if not dynamic, perhaps the greater problem ultimately being the finite number of future opportunities such a model would yield.

3G didn't (*sic*) seek to enhance this model. It sought – and seeks still – to replace it. This was necessarily so because almost everything about the next generation telecoms world is fundamentally different. Huge swathes of traditional infrastructure are rendered redundant in terms of 3G services meaning that, in order to compete and profit in and from the brave new world, the telco faces (more or less) the challenge and massive expense of completely re-engineering itself overnight, effectively before the first 3G call is even completed. This re-engineering relates to both the company's physical infrastructure (its systems) and its very nature as an organization (its strategy and style of management).

This challenge cannot be under-estimated. Consider its scale in the following terms. As we've noted, the traditional world of voice was straightforward. From a technical perspective, a voice call requires the reservation of a single circuit on the network to complete. During a call, no other activity can take place on that circuit (hence the nature of time and distance billing – how long the circuit itself is reserved being a primary basis of the charge). There are an extremely limited number of partners thus involved in the economics of any one phone call, those being the service provider, the caller, and other telcos involved in routing and terminating the call itself whose share of the revenue would be governed by interconnection agreements.

THE CHANGING NATURE OF TELCO BUSINESS

The 3G world (the "fat" pipe we alluded to earlier) benefits from no such simplicity. One transaction (voice or data) does not require the reservation of a single circuit. In fact, numerous transactions (calls or otherwise) occur over the same pipe simultaneously. If these are data transactions the economics of each will involve not just the caller and the interconnect parties, but also the content providers, financial agents, possibly advertisers and, in some cases, other parties. Each will need its own share of the revenue pie to be accounted for. From the perspective of the telco, the challenge is enormous. Whereas the phone company once simply transported calls and made its money from doing so, the modern phone company may effectively become an agent in the process of telecommunications. Is it, to use an analogy, Railtrack (the company that owns the rail network), or is it a train-operating company (a company which provides the service)? Is it the company that built the Panama Canal, or is it the ships that cruise through it? Does the phone company provide its own content, or does it attract customers by providing branded content from elsewhere? Suffice it to say that the very nature of the business is changing. Furthermore, there is not yet a definitive model as to what it is changing into. To some extent, the answers are necessarily emerging as we go along.

Returning to our microscopic example, for instance, the billing system that for years was optimized to cope only with the limited and straightforward parameters of time and distance is suddenly rendered almost useless in the new world of data (where billing for the value and volume of the content may be required). The circuit switch, the core network element in old style networks is effectively redundant in a data network as a source of usage information (the backbone of the phone bill). In short, 3G demands both completely new network elements (the hardware required to build the network itself), completely new operational and business support systems (the software and hardware items required to manage the telco and its relationship with its customers) and a completely new sales and organizational strategy and philosophy because the core product has fundamentally changed. With data, because the parties to each telecommunications transaction are not limited but, rather, many additional parties are involved, an entirely new business model must be born. And all this in support of a new core product that no one can say, with any degree of certainty, that the market wants (no matter how much the telecoms industry wants you to believe that it does).

It's easy to see the scale of the opportunity and thus easy to see how the feeding frenzy began. Equipment manufacturers on all sides of the equation, from the Ciscos and the Lucents that make much of the enabling hardware to the Nokias and Ericssons that make the consumer handsets to the Convergys and others who make the supporting software, were suddenly faced with the once in a lifetime opportunity afforded by a captive market demanding (and needing) a specific core product. Be the first! Innovate! Deliver the 3G solution and untold riches (as Cisco over a number of years proved) await!

On the other hand, from the mobile telephone company perspective, be ready for 3G or die. Whether giant corporate monoliths or small start-ups, billions were literally made overnight by companies that were successfully able to position themselves on the cusp of the 3G boom. That few of these companies had any idea which services would work, and how they would be managed was a distraction in the race to be able to offer them in the first place. It is the collapse of many of these players that has led to the current recession, as the reality that 3G isn't that straightforward after all has finally dawned.

THE TRIUMPH OF OPTIMISM OVER REALITY

The once wealthy infrastructure behemoths in many cases funded the purchase of their own equipment to telco customers whose actual likelihood of surviving to eventually pay up now appears to have been a triumph of optimism over reality. Balance sheets were temporarily inflated, but the underlying assets were far from secure. These companies did as much, for obvious reasons, to contribute to the momentum of the 3G behemoth as did the telcos themselves who, it now appears, bought the propaganda before thinking about how they'd sell the resultant service on to the consumer. Or even which services they'd sell. Today, whilst many still laud the 3G future, albeit tinged with a little more realism, few can identify exactly which services are likely to emerge, or how and how much you'll pay for them.

In those times, the late 1990s, the telecoms market was quite literally a wild place. As we alluded to in the preface, it was awash with (often self aggrandizing) optimisim and woefully short of self-analysis or logic. Through the stock market, money poured into companies barely beyond their embryonic stages as consumers, too, sought to share in a boom that few really understood. The race was on for newcomers to IPO. Technology stocks were "it", though technology companies themselves appear to have been the main heralds of that particular news along with what passes for the "independent" researchers of the financial markets. Everyone believed the messenger simply because everyone wanted to believe and, in the end, because everyone had to. Those involved in the hype felt they couldn't afford not to continue to perpetuate it.

Ultimately, the telecoms market came thus to resemble a vicious circle. Phone companies merged with and acquired each other for hugely inflated prices as they sought to gain an international footing, positioning themselves with apparently little real strategic understanding of either what they were doing or what they were paying to participate in. The titanic egos of more than one CEO added rows of zeroes to many deals. Equipment providers willingly maintained an illusion because their survival depended on doing so. Consumers funded much of it through the equity markets because, one imagines, they didn't want to miss out either (or their fund managers were no more savvy than anyone else). In very, very simple terms, if enough people say the same thing, it will (at least for some period of time) be taken to be true. And then, in the form of license fees, 3G moved another abrupt degree from fiction to fact.

LICENSING 3G

The approach to licensing the right to provide 3G services was not universal. Each country decided the manner in which its own licenses were handed out and, in retrospect, there is a clear relationship between the size of the fees imposed and the scale of the telecoms bloodbath in many markets at present. The approach to fees is, if nothing else, instructive more about what it tells us about the political psyches of individual countries and their governments as much as anything else.

In abstract terms, license fees could be awarded or auctioned, set at nothing or set at the highest possible price. The government that, at the one extreme, believed that the economic impact of 3G was sufficiently beneficial to its country might distribute the license at no cost to the supposed benefit of both the population and the economy as a whole. The government at the other extreme might take the view that here was an economic opportunity to exploit, that industry (in this case the telecoms industry) might be used as a source of funding for its more general agenda and thus to try to extract as much revenue as possible from the licensing process for the treasury. The awards might be done through a beauty contest (to determine which telcos were best able to provide a 3G service), or simply on the basis of which are willing to pay the most. It seems never to have occurred to some governments that in so doing, the industry itself would be crippled along the way. Such has been the devastating impact of 3G license expenditure allied to the other woes in the market discussed earlier that some now estimate that half of the 3G licenses awarded globally may now never be used, which would mean that US$50 million or more has been spent with absolutely no reward.

The extremes of the system for awarding licenses can be seen by a cursory overview of the global market. The twelve most expensive licenses awarded were all in either the UK or Germany, the next five most expensive all in Italy. Vodaphone, holder of the mother of all 3G licenses, paid $9.4 billion for the (dubious) privilege. Collectively, German licenses brought $45.8 billion to the German treasury, $35.4 billion to the UK treasury, and $10.1 billion to the Italian treasury. The list goes on, and for what?

The license fees, though they may result in a boom for the hospital or school building industries, did little more than provide the winners with the right to spend yet more millions building 3G networks to put the pipes in place. In other words, for $9 billion a company such as Vodafone could secure the right to spend another $9 billion or so to offer a product that nobody could, with absolute certainty, say that the market wanted. Now that the market has collapsed, it's this uncertainty that is persuading many to discard their prized licenses before spending another penny building an equally expensive network, examples of which we'll see in the penultimate chapter of this book.

Competitive phone companies, faced with such staggering costs as those involved with 3G, are now looking to work together and cut costs in order to, slowly, try to make a success of next generation services. They're also, in many cases, trying to re-negotiate license terms and launch deadlines. With so much invested already, the general opinion is that they cannot afford not to, somehow, make it work.

WHO WANTS 3G?

Yet the core 3G question remains: does the consumer want the brave new world? Yes, the new data network is "better" than the old circuit switched one from a technological perspective. It's more flexible. It allows for the transport of "exciting" new services. Its potential for future development is enormous. Yes, mobile commerce will push e-commerce into a new phase of development (though the "success" of e-commerce to date is another questionable issue altogether). Yes, there will be lots of prospective opportunities for service and content providers. But so what? Until the end user can be demonstrated to be willing to both support and pay for 3G services, it seems to us that nothing else really matters.

The personal computer has revolutionized our lives. The "success" of the Internet, in a general sense, is beyond dispute. But do we have to have what amounts to an amalgamation of both incorporated into our telephones, and can we not live without the potential afforded by them while we're on the move? So, 3G will allow you to automate a car wash by dialing a number on your phone and the charge will then appear on your bill. Are you willing to pay more for that, or are you happy to just insert a few coins in the slot as you do now? 3G will allow you to receive video clips of your favourite music act while, presumably, you're on the train to work or in some similar situation. Is that something you really want, and if it is, how much would you be willing to pay?

Our guess is, for many, not much (if anything at all). 3G will have its users, in particular the corporate market which may be attracted by facilities such as videoconferencing or the ability to access a corporate network on the road. It will also attract the few anoraks from all walks of life who are either technophiles for the sake of it or who simply cannot exist independent of the very, very latest news on whatever their chosen passion is. But for most of us, voice and SMS services suffice when it comes to giving us what we need from our telecoms provider. Privately, those in the industry that we respect now tell us that the mass acceptance and usage of 3G services is likely to be, at a minimum, at least ten years away and that is assuming that the first services will reach the consumer within the next few months. We believe that unless the 3G extras are free, or priced very competitively indeed, 3G's impact in the short term is going to be very limited at best. If this proves to be the case, then the telecoms industry may face more trouble ahead as it continues to pay for its own mistakes in the years to come.

CASE STUDY

Marconi

The pages of *The Great Telecoms Swindle* are littered with larger-than-life figures, would-be giants of the corporate landscape. But the names of Winnick, Ebbers, McGinn and their ilk have already been revealed to be creations of little more than ego and bluster, image with little underlying substance. These men were opportunists, at best.

If the measure of a business titan is simply the ability to achieve personal enrichment, then a great many Mount Rushmore's may be carved in the memory and to the glorification of those pied pipers who led the telecoms market into the abyss. What is sad, even tragic, is that in doing so they destroyed, in some cases, the legacies of real business giants, and the great companies they created in the process. Such is the story of the fall of Marconi in which one of Britain's great industrial success stories was more or less utterly destroyed. The story of Marconi's downfall is representative of our age . . . the life work of a "dull", conservative genius who built something of tangible and lasting value reduced to ruins by the ill-informed doings of a modernist, supposedly media-genic incompetent capable of little more than attaching himself to the first bandwagon that passed.

Marconi, before its ill-fated excursion into telecoms, had been a true industrial giant, respected globally for its reputation in engineering and with a notional value of some £35 billion. The company had been known as GEC and its development and pre-eminent position in British commerce had been achieved through the work and leadership of Arnold (Lord) Weinstock, who had been at the company's helm for 33 years. He had a created a business which had made profits of £981 million and had a £1.4 billion cash pile.

Weinstock's secrets were as different from those espoused as keys to success during the modern age as night is from day. He was cautious, conservative, and hardworking. Reflecting his approach, GEC was diverse, unglamorous, and steady; a conglomeration of interests including Hotpoint, Yarrow Shipbuilders, Metropolitan Vickers, Avery, and The Marconi Company. Weinstock navigated those interests successfully through nine changes of government, six recessions, and more on an unwavering course which benefited the company, his shareholders and, indeed, the economy alike. He has, not accidentally, been described as one of the greatest industrialists of our age.

When Weinstock finally stepped down, he was replaced by a man who would prove as incompetent as he was able, one George Simpson, often described by the press as a "golf loving Scot" (who should, perhaps, have stayed on the golf course). It is hard to imagine, though perhaps an incidental note, Weinstock ever being described in such terms but amidst the boom that preceded the crash, the order of the day in the telecoms world was for whiz-kids, big personalities, colour, and hype.

It was Simpson who, as chief executive, devised the strategy that was to annihilate the foundations of an industrial giant.

Where Weinstock had been cautious and deliberate, Simpson was instantly bold. He sold off GEC's defence business in short order, then renamed the company Marconi and set about spending Weinstock's accumulated cash mountain in the booming telecoms market. For a very short time, the strategy worked as investors (as we now know) erroneously seized on any telecoms-related opportunity with a vengeance. Within almost no time at all, however, Marconi was struggling for nothing other than basic survival.

Today, Simpson's creation is expected to make an operating loss this year of almost £100 million – before goodwill write-offs of up to £3.5 billion on a series of acquisitions. Its debt stands at £4.4 billion. Only a conditional loan agreement amongst its bankers is keeping the company operational. Simpson, the man who arrived at GEC (from a car manufacturer) with a promise to "open the windows" and "jerk up earnings" is long since gone. In Britain, he is the face of the Telecoms Swindle.

Simpson had clearly arrived expecting to impose both himself and a personal vision on GEC. He hired a contrary but capable city banker, John Mayo, to work alongside him as finance director and, in 1998 and 1999 he decided his deliberately denuded GEC would become a key player in the telecoms equipment market. He saw, as we have illustrated, the Internet taking off and the number of telcos being created across Europe and, never mind that he appeared neither to have understood nor adequately investigated the market, this was going to be his and Marconi's road to greatness.

Simpson's asset sales raised around £3 billion dollars, headed by the sale of GEC's defence business to British Aerospace in a deal which put £2.7 billion cash into the company's coffers. He had every intention of rapidly putting that money to work.

Simpson's company spent £4.1 billion buying two US network equipment manufacturers and, in November 1999 GEC renamed itself Marconi, "Europe's brightest technology company" though not run by Europe's brightest technology people. The press and the financial markets bowed down before Simpson's bold approach, though it now belatedly appears that he had little understanding of the business he was entering.

By 1991, as we have seen, the tide in the industry had turned and Marconi's rivals and customers alike were openly admitting that a recession had arrived. Simpson's company, rather like an ostrich, publicly buried its head in the sand and appeared to completely ignore both the obvious and the inevitable. At one stage, Mayo described a market which was crashing in increasingly spectacular fashion as going through a "pause period". Even in 2002, Simpson was confident that profits would grow and nothing was amiss. In truth, it beggars belief both that anyone would have the effrontery to make such claims in the face of widespread evidence to the contrary and, perhaps even more, that anyone else would believe them.

Inevitably, the crash reached Marconi and for its troubles in refusing to recognize and admit to the state of the industry earlier, its fall was made all the more spectacular. On the morning of July 4th 2001, the company requested its shares be suspended pending a trading statement which would be made after the stock market had closed. The statement – unheard of for a company of Marconi's size – announced (out of the blue) that profits would halve and 4,000 redundancies would be added to the 3,000 already recently announced.

Within a day, Marconi's share price had halved. Within a week, Mayo had taken on the role of first sacrifical lamb and been forced out.

The problems were, however, only beginning. If anyone thought Simpson's announcement was the bottom of the curve, they were to be proved sorely wrong. Customer spending was still slowing and millions of pounds of equipment Marconi had built was piling up unused. As cash was drained for operational expenses, more layoffs ensued. At the subsequent board meeting, with new financial reports indicating that the future would become bleaker yet, the board of directors concluded that enough was enough. Simpson (and his chairman Sir Roger Hurn) were despatched, the former publicly unapologetic for his "achievements".

By the following November, three months later, Marconi was announcing losses of £5.1 billion for the first half of the financial year, compared to a loss of just £66 million the previous twelve months. Seven thousand jobs had by then been slashed. A further reduction of 3,000 was tabled. Marconi admitted it was considering the sale of £100 million of property to help reduce its debts, issuing a further profits warning in the process.

The folly of Simpson's vision had been thoroughly betrayed.

Today, Marconi stands on the brink of oblivion. It has reached agreement with its financiers on a financial restructuring that effectively forgives £4 billion of its debts and leaves previous shareholders with just a 0.5 percent stake in a new Marconi Corporation. The deal had taken the majority of the first half of 2002 to negotiate, and shareholders will have no say in its acceptance. The future of the company lies in the hands of the banks. It intends to relist itself, in 2003, on both the London stock exchange and the NASDAQ.

If the deal is completed, the new company expects to have enough cash to trade through the continuing telecoms market downturn, albeit as a shadow of its former self. It expects the telecoms market to begin to recover by the end of 2003 and to turn an operating profit in the course of the following year. The new, scaled-down Marconi will concentrate only on very specific market niches.

Whatever Marconi becomes, it will likely take decades if it is even ever possible for the company to reach anything near its former position as one of Britain's pre-eminent industrial powers. Quite simply, the scale of the telecoms crash is perhaps more clearly illustrated than anywhere else in its humbling of this corporate giant. George Simpson has taken on the image of a universal buffoon. Unlike Winnick and others he was no whiz-kid, sharp, savvy, and aware of a quick profit when he saw one or a market about to boom. He created nothing, and wasn't even part of the launch of the roller-coaster when some might have been forgiven for thinking the opportunities really were as good as they seemed. Simpson was a bandwagon jumper who chased the pack when the wheels were already starting to come off, with little apparent clue of his own limitations in doing so. He slunk off into the sunset surreptitiously offering, for the most part, the hundreds of investors whose savings he had ignorantly frittered away the immortal explanation: "no comment". Therein lies another prominent facet of the Great Telecoms Swindle.

CHAPTER 6

The state we're in

Re-engineering the telco

Whether or not 3G itself is the dominant future medium, broadband, IP, fat-pipe technologies are the future basis of the telecoms industry. The transfer to such network backbones is ongoing and, in fact, investment in the design and build of these networks has already evolved into a major headache within the telecoms market. As with all bandwagons when everyone jumps on at once, there are soon too many for the road to accommodate.

In the simple and traditional world of telecoms to which we keep alluding, phone companies owned and built networks made up, essentially, of copper wires in the ground managed by circuit switches, devices to direct traffic over the network and sited at local exchanges. Before competition, therefore, telephone companies were fundamentally engineering organizations whose primary concern was the maintenance and management of a network and for whom, in relative terms, the customer (a captive audience before competition was introduced) needed only to be serviced by the provision of a working service. In very simple terms, the telco employed a lot of engineers and a few customer-facing representatives to handle any problems that arose.

In the new telecoms world, not only is the phone company entirely different by nature, but there is no such thing as a "phone company" at all, at least in so far as no one catch all phrase exists to describe *all* the businesses that can claim in one way or another to be the domain of phone companies. In the industry at present, there is a sea of acronyms to describe the various niches into which players pigeonhole themselves. The key distinctions within the market are that providers of telecoms services no longer necessarily own physical networks themselves (so some are known as "virtual" telcos of which, in the UK at least, Virgin mobile is the best known), and that companies that do build and manage networks no longer necessarily provide services to the end user (you or I). These companies are sometimes known as "carrier's carriers", and they simply design and build modern network, recouping their costs by leasing space to the service providers who in turn serve the end-user customer.

It is in the carrier's carrier market, perhaps predictably, that another root of the present crisis can be found. As became apparent in the 1990s, the future of the circuit switched network was limited due to the flexibility and capacity of IP-based broadband networks (the fat pipe technologies) and so the opportunity arose for a new kind of telco business.

PAYING FOR BANDWIDTH INFRASTRUCTURE

Traditional operators, perhaps wincing at the prospect of a two-pronged demand on their resources (network build plus the need, in the wake of liberalization, to compete and thus to become customer-responsive organizations), increasingly sought to defray the cost of the wires in the ground side of the business. This was particularly true for the new competitive operators who did not come into existence with physical networks of their own and whose advantage over the former incumbents (who, such as BT, did own the networks upon which they were reliant) was that they were customer facing, slick marketing organizations already. These operators, wanting to play to their strengths, did not want to become engineering companies. It wasn't the future anyway, and it certainly wasn't their core skill.

Partly as a result of the need for engineering companies, the carrier's carrier was born. These companies, such as Carrier One, Global Crossing, and others anticipated the demand for broadband network capacity and invested in the design, build, and management of new, often global, IP networks. Their expense would be offset, and their profits would come from leasing capacity to the new competitive carrier market. It was, prospectively, a win–win situation. In simple terms, carrier's carriers would become the engineering side of the telecoms business, and competitive telcos the marketing side. Everyone would do, theoretically, what they were good at. Everyone would reap the rewards. As it was assumed that demand for the basic commodity, bandwidth, was unlimited, the recipe appeared to be "can't miss"!

So in theory at least, the idea behind such businesses wasn't a bad one. In practice with, once again, investors and bankers pouring in cash on a wave of blind optimism as much as any realistic projections, the market ended up underwriting a predicted demand for capacity that was never remotely likely to exist. State-of-the-art fibre cables were laid, quite literally, around the globe at huge expense. Demand for capacity on these newly created networks never came. In fact, demand didn't even come close. In short, Carrier One, Global Crossing, WorldCom and many of their counterparts found themselves with miles and miles of "dark fibre" on their hands (laid cable that is never likely to be "switched on" or lit up). The carrier's carrier market, as we shall see, paid a heavy price.

The broadband glut not only drove many of the companies directly behind the new networks into the ground but, inevitably, it had a disastrous effect on the economics of the telecoms market due to its impact on pricing. When (*sic*) there's too much of anything the price drops. When there's much too much, it goes through the floor. For this reason, amongst others, the network builders soon had little prospect of recouping their investment, not that in a limited sense this was necessarily a bad thing for the telecoms customer.

In theory, the excess of network capacity was advantageous from the consumer's perspective. The competitive carrier market boomed (more competing telcos fighting increasingly desperate battles for customers) but the battle was being waged, increasingly, on shifting ground. The raw materials, in the form of capacity, were plentiful but the opportunity to turn them into profits (through customers) was becoming increasingly difficult.

DIVERGING DISCIPLINES

The customer, in the new telecoms world, is the battleground upon which the war for supremacy is being fought. As we noted earlier, there was a time when telcos were fundamentally in the business of network engineering but, as the network evolved and liberalization took hold, the business became one of marketing and customer service.

The two disciplines (customer-facing and network-facing) have little in common and this is one of many reasons why in spite of their built in advantage as owners of the network, former incumbents like BT have manifestly struggled in recent years. Ownership of the local loop and, as such, the ability to reap the benefits of interconnection provided security in the short term, but in the long term the benefits dissipate and, without a new strategic vision and, more importantly, the ability to execute it, even former giants have proved vulnerable to struggle.

At this point, it's worth returning briefly to an examination of the old and the new telecoms networks since it is from the wires themselves that everything else springs. The reader will remember that the old, circuit switched network operated on a relatively simple economic model with limited participants in each transaction and proven reliability in engineering terms.

The new, IP-based network (essentially an Internet-type network) operates entirely differently. Because of its flexibility and capacity, the telco has the ability to re-invent itself as a new sort of organization, one which offers a variety of services rather than a single deliverable good. Thus, whereas on the old network price and price alone could be the basis for competition (in theory, the telco that offered the lowest price for a voice call might be expected to win the most customers and thus the greatest market share), in the broadband world there are any number of prospective areas for competition.

In terms of 3G, for instance, quality or variety of content might prove to be more important than price alone, the ability not just to get something cheaply but to get the desired quality too. Suddenly, the telco had become the retailer rather the manufacturer, with all the different challenges such a shift in focus involves.

WHOSE CUSTOMER AM I?

The key questions, and for telcos these were entirely new, became how to win customers, how to retain them and, the question that might ultimately prove most important of all, who actually owns the customer? If, for instance, you receive news bulletins from *The Times* over your Orange phone, are you a customer of Orange, or are you a customer of *The Times*? This question, which will be discussed in more detail later in this chapter, is absolutely critical. At the present moment it remains largely unanswered, which suggests that the future of the telco from an investment perspective must remain entirely unclear. We can, and many do, talk about when the recession will end but even if it ended tomorrow, there is no degree of certainty about the landscape that would emerge. In fact, we believe that until the picture of the nature of the telco's business becomes clearer, confidence in the market is unlikely to return in full. There's still a long way to go before that is the case.

The modern telco is, then, involved in a number of disciplines and it has a number of opportunities from which to profit in addition to challenges to overcome in order to do so. If the telco is a former incumbent, what position does it take with regard to its network; what role does the local loop (the last mile of cable between the local exchange and the customers home) play in its future? As OFTEL has broadly whittled down BT's control over its exchanges, allowing its competitors ever freer access to the end user, the notion of BT simply selling its local loop business appears to have been considered and, for the moment, rejected.

Arguments against such a sale involve the loss of a still prized asset. Those who argue in favour would claim that now is the time to cash in and, in any event, doing so would enhance BT's prospects of re-inventing itself and focusing firmly on the new ball of being a customer-focused organization. Whether or not BT has made the right decision, or even what the right decision might be is open to question, but that such issues have clouded the organization's sense of purpose and understanding of itself is probably beyond debate. Developing the right strategy takes time enough. Developing a coherent understanding of your organization in a revolutionary climate is harder yet.

Almost certainly, the successful telcos of the future will be fundamentally marketing and customer service led organizations though that is not to say that they will be either network independent or "virtual" in nature (in all probability, when normal service is fully resumed, the opposite will be the case). The likelihood is also, at some point, that the market will contract to the extent that it will come to resemble at least in passing the telecoms industry as it existed before liberalization, though the new "incumbents" will operate on a global rather than a local scale. The correct selection of these prospective new incumbents is one attractive avenue for investment in the telecoms market at present though it may be harder to find the right horses than it sounds.

This contraction will happen simply because the market cannot support the number of players vying for the customers attention at present. Customers exist in finite numbers, and ultimately the means to attract them is rigid too. Whether a drop in price (usually temporary), innovation in service terms (such as pay-as-you-go), or innovation in offering (the data services we may yet see soon), experience to date indicates that it is relatively easy to win customers, but extremely difficult to retain them.

THE COST OF ACQUIRING A CUSTOMER BASE

The nature of any subscription business is that each customer comes with an acquisition cost (the cost of bringing that customer on board). This cost is usually not fully recouped until some time into the relationship and, therefore, if a new customer joins up in response to an attractive offer but moves on shortly thereafter to another attractive offer from a competitor, the business would in some cases have been better off never having had that customer in the first place. The telecoms industry term for this rolling over of customer rosters is "churn", and dealing with churn is a critical pre-occupation for service providers at present.

Put simply, it is arguable that at the present time many domestic markets have more competing telcos than can realistically be supported (the mobile market in Britain is one prime example). The result is that ever more attractive offers are put out to win fininite numbers of customers, relatively few of whom are retained after the initial period. However, in order to paint a more encouraging picture (and in order not to discourage critical flows of investment) the industry itself keeps its subscriber figures a closely guarded secret. Inactive accounts (those which have been unused for months, wherein the customer has left the network in all but name) are counted among subscriber numbers, and actual churn statistics are zealously protected from view. The picture the telco paints of itself is often not what it seems.

The problem herein lies in the fact that even the slickest of marketing cannot overcome the constraints and dictates of economic reality. Brand building (Orange being a case in point) is undoubtably critical as a factor in success in the new telecoms world, but brand building without scale and in an uncertain economy are not, alone, enough. France Telecom paid way over the odds for the Orange brand while the industry was riding high. Now a fire sale is likely as the brand alone has proved not enough. In many cases, the best of goods have been revealed as damaged upon closer inspection. Plus, in the rush to expand at all costs, post-expansion strategy was all too often overlooked.

One key result of the struggle for numerical ascendancy in terms of customer base has been the internationalization of the market. With finite opportunities at home, telcos have inevitably sought growth abroad in the quest for profit. Again too often the approach to doing so has been self-defeatingly simplistic . . . buy now, think later. As key sales have increasingly taken on the mantle of auctions (Telecom Italia and Mannesman, to name but two) in which prices have been horribly exaggerated for what have almost appeared to be reasons of ego, little thought has been given either to the real-world economic impact of such deals or to the role of the purchases post acquisition. At the same time highly touted partnerships (such as Concert, the joint venture between BT and AT&T) have been entered into and, subsequently, dissolved amidst a welter of failed expectations.

In light of the complexity of telecoms' new world order, and the demands that transitioning to a new type of business would inevitably place on service providers, it is perhaps not entirely surprising that the Great Telecoms Swindle has taken shape. One might think that any one of re-engineering one's company, re-building one's core product, establishing oneself in a newly competitive market, and seeking to expand within that market, would be challenge enough at any one time. To attempt to reach all four goals simultaneously, it could be argued was an intention bordering on the suicidal from the start. That the price presently being paid is high should, in reality, come as no surprise to anyone though the heroic stupidity of many decision-makers continues to elicit a certain amount of awe.

None more so, and few stories are more instructive, than that of Marconi about which more detail is given in a case study. Once, as GEC, it was the backbone performer of British industry and run with knife-edge precision and a keen, conservative fiscal intelligence by Arnold (Lord) Weinstock as a diverse yet focused conglomerate of businesses with a cash pile of £1.4 billion. Upon Weinstock's retirement George Simpson, his successor, sought to reinvent the company in the late 1990s as a telecoms network equipment provider. What followed was a meltdown of epic proportions.

Simpson, it would appear, knew little more about the telecoms market than he might have read in the press or, even worse, the trade press which, at the time, amounted to the glossy fact that telecoms was the self-proclaimed place to be. Shedding more or less everything that has made GEC what it was, Simpson bought the press release hook, line, and sinker, buying telecoms properties with a vigour that bordered on the belligerent, paying whatever it took, re-naming Marconi in the process and turning the cash pile he'd inherited into an equally sizeable debt. It took around two years for the bubble to burst, and when it burst it did so spectacularly. Today, Marconi is a shell of its former self, dependent on the largesse of its bankers to survive even in a form that is a meagre in the context of its former glories. Acquisitions for which it paid billions are now worth pennies. Simpson, now departed, has said little but he has, at any rate, declined to say that his venture into telecoms was in any way fundamentally wrong.

AUGURIES OF DISASTER

It was, in fact, the network equipment market that was in many ways the first to go and its waning performance the first to augur the depth of the oncoming disaster. During the feeding frenzy of the late 1990s, all too often equipment manufacturers propped up their telco customers in the expectation of recouping their investments as the market expanded and competitive players took root.

Newly licensed operators in increasingly unlikely corners of the globe clearly had little money during their nascent period, so to win their long-term business the equipment manufacturers increasingly "partnered" with them, providing loans to purchase their equipment or, more cynically but accurately as it has often turned out, giving their equipment away for free. That smaller or start-up telecoms suppliers should act in this way in order to establish the efficacy of their products is, perhaps, not surprising, but that established behemoths such as Lucent should be brought to their knees by similar mismanagement beggars belief. The collapse of Lucent (again, more detail is given in one of our case studies) was, perhaps, the first big name fall in the present catastrophe. The fact that it should happen to a company that could be reasonably described as the grandfather of the NEPs (network equipment providers) suggested the scale of the collapse to come.

THE FALL OF THE HOUSE OF LUCENT

Lucent's demise, in some ways, mirrored the problems that its telco customers themselves were facing. Once the network engineering arm of the former US incumbent but spun off as an independent entity when the Baby Bells were created, the jewel in Lucent's considerable crown was Bell Labs, for years *the* research and development lab of more or less the entire telecoms industry. Whether advanced signalling systems, developments in network engineering or otherwise, chances were that great leaps forward in telecoms had their roots somewhere behind Bell Labs doors where its impressive repository of Nobel prize-winning scientists worked.

But Lucent in the mid-to-late-1990s faced many similar problems to those of the telcos. Its reputation was that of master of the voice world and its core business remained rooted in the circuit switched network. In the new world towards which the market was moving, Cisco had usurped and then rapidly consolidated its position as the dominant player on the block.

Lucent had neither strong leadership (and, as we subsequently found out, poorer leadership than we understood at the time), vision nor strategy and was encumbered by the former incumbent's mentality and organizational set-up which restricted its effectiveness in reacting to the market changes taking place around it. Lucent was unable to transition to the new network world with any sense of purpose or any real sense of its destiny. It acquired companies to expand its offering at sometimes frighteningly inflated prices, then seemed not to have any real of what to do with them once they were on board. It was a familiar story, and the profit warnings that followed were inevitable.

The general reader will, reasonably, ask the question, "but surely someone must have known what was going on?" How could an entire, billion dollar industry fall off a mountain overnight? Why was there so little warning? Why was cash being poured into telecoms stock quite literally up to the metaphorical day before the wheels came off the track?

In our opinion, a combination of arrogance, ignorance,

wilfulness and momentum are to blame. The Swindle about which we write is not primarily so much a matter of deceipt as a matter of stupidity on a quite literally epic scale. It may yet be proved that fraud or illegal accounting tactics played some role in keeping sinking ships afloat as long as was the case, but the underlying reality was the reason that so many leaks had been sprung in the first place. There was likely no crime in the period of expansion which fuelled the collapse, only mismanagement on the grandest of scales. And further mismanagement as the walls started to crumble inwards.

In many ways, it is not surprising that the Great Telecoms Swindle was exposed so suddenly, but that it took as long as it did for the collapse to happen. Even a cursory evaluation of balance sheets or a cursory knowledge of the likely real value of players within the market should have made even the minimally informed feel uneasy. When an acquistion is made at a price that appears to bear no relationship to reality, questions need to be asked. None, however, were asking them.

We remember speaking to the CEO of a company whose leading competitor was acquired by Lucent and laughing openly about the price. We asked him if he would like to go "on the record" with a comment and his response was something to the effect that we must be kidding. So what if the deal verged on the insane, think what the company he'd founded was worth now! Incidentally, it's worth today about 10 percent of what it was worth then, and, ironically, it is probably more successful, better established, and with a more impressive customer base than it had at that time. Such is the world of telecoms.

HIDING THE PROBLEMS

The point is, the market became a "closed shop". When both the supplier and the customer and the competition are in the same boat, all propping up the other and with no one in position to provide strong or visionary leadership for the market as a whole, human nature is such that safety will be sought in numbers. If everyone sticks to the script, perhaps the extent of real-world problems will never be uncovered by outsiders. And of the "outsiders" (and we use the term in the loosest sense of the word) whose business it was to poke their noses into the telecoms market as arbiters of financial sense and future prospects (the investment analysts), that community proved itself collectively more inept than the worst of the telecoms CEOs. In a five year period, we must have read analysis of the balance sheets of literally hundreds of companies from this source. We are hard pressed to think of a single instance where anything less than a "buy" recommendation was made in reference to telecom stocks. It is almost hard to muster any sympathy at all for the investor who chooses to rely on this community for guidance in making decisions.

In short, the telecoms world had, by mid 2000, brought itself to its knees. It was populated by service providers servicing nothing so much as mountains of debt and doing so on the back of often unprofitable investments and increasingly reliant on the provision of a new services world which wasn't taking shape anywhere near as quickly as projected and the customer response to which would be uncertain, at best. Allied to these were equipment providers whose own debt was often being propped up from beneath by nothing more than the debt of their customers. A fever of acquisitions in both the service provider and supplier markets had left a raft of large, unwieldy, and increasingly directionless companies sitting on dwindling balance sheets, listing in the wind. Even the hardware required for the launch of new services (2.5 and 3G handsets, for example) had not arrived as predicted.

As if that wasn't enough, initial forays into the data world had proved inconclusive at best and abjectly disappointing at worst. WAP, the first pure post-2G step into the mobile Internet, was much heralded by some in the industry but proved to be an irrelevance for all but the few who indulged. Arguably useful albeit limited in end-user offerings at times but unattractive and, to be generous, functional it was anything but an eye catching-move in the battle to convince the customer that a telecoms-dependant future was secure. GPRS, the bigger step towards the mobile Internet and a more 3G-like advance in pure terms was long promised but, across Europe, it has still not for the most part arrived.

A cynical response would inevitably build up amongst consumers for whom only SMS services had been adopted with a passion and, for all the success of that medium, short messages alone were not enough to achieve the revolution that had been promised. Within the industry, revisionist historians on all sides dismissed WAP on the one hand ("wait until you see what's coming next") and at the same time argued that it had been a more successful endeavour from a revenue perspective than you might think on the other. It was, simultaneously, a success and a failure. Either way, a firework display it was not though that didn't prevent some from attempting to have their cake and eat it.

Something had to give, and it was inevitable that something would.

It is, in reality, not at all surprising that it was the giants on all sides of the equation that gave. Whilst many of the smaller, competitive carriers struggled and sank, it was the sudden demise of the highlights in late 2001 and early 2002 that brought the reality and extent of the crisis home to bear. On the carrier side, US giant WorldCom imploded amidst (*sic*) the ongoing flurry of accounting scandals. The nature of these, as we shall see later, is instructive in understanding the state of the broader market.

The carrier's carrier, Global Crossing, strangled itself in self-built rings of dark fibre. Directionless Lucent (*sic*), keeling over, started a fire sale of assets in a desperate attempt to survive. Marconi presently clings to life, but may well yet go under. The personalities who, in the boom days, cried havoc and let loose the dogs of a budgetary war are now largely gone. To their successors has been bequeathed the task of restoring not just order but sanity to a market that lost any sense of itself.

The greater miracle is, in many ways, that it took so long to reach the state we're in today.

CHAPTER 7

The perfect storm

The boom goes bust

Taken separately, each of the threads that woven together created the bright tapestry known as the new telecoms market by 1999, collectively augured for an exciting future for all concerned. This was an industry built on optimism, confidence, innovation and a sense that nothing could go wrong.

As a result, money poured into telecoms, share prices soared, millionaires were made overnight as successful IPO followed successful IPO and companies in all corners of the market announced little but good news. Corporate giants who weren't already involved in telecoms sought to move urgently into the space. The financial markets devoured every optimistic projection thrown at them and, unquestioningly for a time, opened their purses again and again. But the telecoms bubble was, in fact, about to burst in spectacular fashion.

Its collapse, especially in the early stages, was overshadowed by the largely simultaneous fall of the dotcom market which, though far smaller and less significant was perhaps the more obvious "glamour" industry of the day and thus attention was deflected from the extent of the telecoms problem to hand in the early stages of the fall. In truth, dot.bomb was small fry, as the world was about to find out. Between 1997 and 2001 it is estimated that more than $4,000 billion dollars were spent on telecoms equipment and services in Europe and the United States. The collapse of such an investment was to be far more than a minor bump on the general economic road.

What was actually at stake, where the health of the telecoms market was concerned, was little short of staggering. The Financial Times has stated that between 1996 and 2001, banks agreed $890 billion in syndicated loans. A further $415 billion of debt was drawn from bond markets and $500 billion from private equity and stock market issuance. Even more money came from the likes of Marconi, blue chip companies that in the belief that telecoms was a "can't-miss" proposition turned cash piles into massive pools of debt in pursuit of a piece of the action.

By 1999 around half of bank lending in Europe was directed to sources related to the telecoms industry. Over three quarters of all junk bonds issued in the US were telco-derived. Five of the ten largest mergers in corporate history up to that point in time involved phone companies. Put very simply, if the telecoms market collapsed, it wasn't go to go down alone and it wasn't going to go down quietly. Still, no one seemed worried that anything could go wrong.

BLIND OPTIMISM

In truth, the prospect of serious problems or worse simply were barely even considered by many who should have know better. The blind optimism that we encountered in that period (and, in fairness, which we did not always question then) seems laughable today. The over-riding sense was that business planning was a matter of dreaming the most expansive dreams you could because the cash would be there to fund their transformation into reality. With money so easy to come by, the industry simply came to believe its own hype. For banks and telcos alike, the telecoms market was little more than a license to print money.

And yet, within less than eighteen months after 1999, the pendulum had swung dramatically to the other extreme. It turned out that the money pouring into the industry had been used to buy the emperor not so much a set of new clothes as an entire wardrobe.

And what was in that wardrobe? For a start, bandwidth (and copious quantities of it at that) was everywhere you looked. Bandwidth – fibre optic cable which in many cases had been built but never lit up – was probably as responsible as anything in the end for turning out the lights on the entire telecoms boom.

BANDWIDTH OVERCAPACITY

Bandwidth is the raw material required to transmit volumes of data across communications networks. As such, it is the raw material of telecoms itself. Bandwidth is to telecoms what roads are to the transportation industry. During the course of the boom, huge amounts of money were invested in increasing the availability of bandwidth, effectively building new roads in anticipation of cars that were certain to use them. Building and owning networks was thus literally to be at the head of the gold-rush.

Yet, by 2001 there was such a severe glut of bandwidth that it was estimated that 6 billion people could talk continuously on the telephone for a year and their calls could be transmitted over the capacity available within a few hours. Less than 4 percent of the fibre optic cable that had been laid (and financed) during the boom had even been activated. (There is now a real possibility it may remain "dark" permanently. It is, for now, simply not needed.)

You might well ask, how could the industry have got it so wrong? To overbuild by 5 or 10 percent might suggest a mixture of poor judgement and bad luck. To overbuild by 95 to 98 percent suggests little more than a combination of ignorance and wrecklessness. Oh, and greed. In chasing miracles, the bandwidth builders simply lost the plot.

With such a glut of capacity, what happened next was easy to predict; the price of bandwidth collapsed. Already debt-laden companies (such as WorldCom) who had fuelled the explosion were now sitting on what were effectively almost totally worthless assets, investments which would likely never return anything near their original value. At the same time, mobile phone companies were indulging in a bandwidth explosion of their own, committing over $200 billion to boost their brand of bandwidth and thus enable wireless Internet services for which (see chapter 5) there was not even any hard evidence of consumer demand.

This excess of bandwidth was the straw that broke the camel's back. Essentially, it exposed the fact that the telecoms economy was a false one and contradicted the basic balances of supply and demand. It was the same story across other segments of the market. The industry had been funded at countless levels to create product for which there was little evidence of need. There was a domino effect; if this happens, that will happen, and that will happen, but with the bandwidth glut the first domino was never knocked over. "Progress" had become self perpetuating, change anticipated on the basis of what "could" be done, rather than what anyone needed to do.

THE FALSE ECONOMY

Just how false was the false economy? At the height of the boom in 2000, the stock market value of all telecoms related businesses was in the region of $6,300 billion. Within a year, it had virtually halved. Billions of dollars of loans were in default. Half a million people had lost their jobs in the course of the crisis. Countless telecoms operators had filed for bankruptcy, having built networks which now, to all intents and purposes, have barely any value at all.

Perhaps a salutary tale should have been the fate of Iridium, a multi-billion dollar satellite communications network launched by Motorola in 1997, before the telecoms crash. To us, the Iridium story is redolent of what the 3G story may yet become. Iridium, put simply, would deliver mobile communications anytime, anywhere so that (somewhat clunky handset notwithstanding) you could, were you so minded, telephone a colleague in the Sahara desert whilst standing on top of Everest (at a price). Someone, somewhere, thought there would be massive demand for such versatility and flexibility (possibly the same person who now thinks that large chunks of the population will find it impossible to live without 3G services by the end of the first quarter, 2003).

Guess what? Within three years Iridium had collapsed with scarcely a nominal amount of customers to its name. They gave a party . . . nobody came. Its satellites were to be abandoned . . . left to crash back to earth before the US Department of Defense bought them from the bankruptcy court for, wait for it, only £25 million.

Those dramatic losses are part of a trend that now runs throughout the industry. It is generally estimated that, when the bankruptcy courts have completed their business, perhaps 10 percent of the costs of the network building programmes of the 1990s will be recouped in the fire sale of assets that is in the process of taking place. When you add in the additional losses (the spending on infrastructure, people, and otherwise) that number is reduced even further. How did it come to this?

As we've said, during the boom years it was apparent that the telco market believed it had a fail-safe formula for success. Deregulation had introduced a swathe of new-breed, competitive companies into the fixed line market, and the mobile explosion was not only turning in what appeared to be ever-more impressive numbers but, with the potential of the Internet in the offing, revenues were seen as certain to increase.

Voice telephony made money . . . the Internet offered the opportunity to make exponentially more.

Network building (bandwidth – *sic*) became a further end in itself. And this top line optimism rapidly filtered down to the supporting infrastructure markets, where in anticipation of the changes in usage patterns and the demands made by the prospective arrival of online commerce, solutions on both the hardware and software sides were soon in equally high demand, thus fuelling a boom in the telecoms support sector proportional in scale to the boom in the telecoms market itself.

Telcos sought to re-invent themselves and they needed to restructure their internal landscapes to support the new vision. Where they didn't anticipate what needed re-inventing to reach this goal, eager suppliers were only too happy to tell them. The blind, in short order, came to lead the blind, selling each other products they scarcely needed, rarely used effectively, but ownership of which nonetheless fit the master plan of progress.

If the bandwidth glut, as we alluded to earlier, was the first straw to break the camel's back and weaken the foundation of the market as a whole, it was probably the issue of 3G licenses which did the same for the mobile side of the market and thus sent the industry collectively finally spiralling out of control. How bad was the misjudgement where these licenses was concerned? To give but one example, Sonera of Finland, amongst other operators, spent $109 billion on them and later gave one back for free rather than add to the money it had already spent (four billion euros).

A SWINDLE OF INCOMPETENCE

As we've said throughout this book, in our view the Great

Telecoms Swindle is not so much a swindle of malfeasance or criminal behaviour as a swindle of sheer and absolute incompetence on the part of industry leaders. It is at this point that the fundamental question can and must be asked: how did these people get everything so absolutely wrong? How could apparently intelligent and successful businessmen at the peak of their careers so wholly misjudge both the essence of their companies, the nature of the markets in which they were active, and the needs of their customers. Furthermore, how could they induce the financial world to underwrite their idiotic beliefs?

There is another way of putting this question, and it exposes the raw emotion that underlies the collapse. The web is littered with first-hand tales of the fallout of the Swindle, penned by ex-telecoms employees whose lives have been shattered by the events we describe. One of those, indirectly, raises the same questions on the website Global Double Crossing.com:

> Today, I read an article in *USA Today*. In it, it had a heart-warming story about how your [Gary Winnick – CEO of the company] daughter said that a lot of bad stories were being written about you but "I still love you daddy." Let me tell you something, asshole.
>
> I have two twin daughters that I have to look at every day, knowing I invested in your company and was planning for their future based on your fucking lies. I could have accepted that I'd made a bad decision if you hadn't stated that there was no bankruptcy in GX's future and that GX was ok for 2002. But no, puppet

> master, you lied. If you had been truthful and said the company was in trouble that would have been a different thing. But now I, along with a shitload of other good people are fucked.
>
> . . . I am so sorry your daughter has to keep listening to people calling you a piece of shit.

The point being, the Great Telecoms Swindle is not only a story about incompetent power brokers and how they achieved self-immolation in the manner they did. It's about the wider impact that events which often seem impersonal have had on thousand of lives.

ARROGANCE, IGNORANCE, HUBRIS

To be absolutely honest, the question "how could it happen?" is not easy to answer. How can a combination of arrogance, ignorance, and hubris on a multi-billion dollar scale be explained? Where do you find the logic behind writing a £5 billion cheque simply for the right to build and provide a service that there is scarcely a single shred of hard evidence that anybody wants? If the question is to be answered, we need to continue looking at how the tidal wave was generated.

Perhaps not surprisingly in the context of modern industry, the figure who (entirely unwittingly) inspired the race into oblivion was Bill Gates who, in 1995, gave a presentation that argued, very simply, that the Internet would create a massive demand for bandwidth. During the early 1990s, the Internet's appeal had broadened beyond its origins as a scientific tool and its potential as a medium of mass communication, if it could be further developed and adapted, had become clear to Microsoft's leader at least.

Gates' presentation was absorbed by one Walter Scott, then chairman of a long-distance US operator called MFS, a competitor of AT&T. Buying into Gates' vision, Scott saw an opportunity and promptly sold MFS. He used the proceeds for a new company, called Level 3 Communications which was to effectively enact the Gatesian vision. It was Level 3 that, to all intents and purposes, turned the "hot" telecoms industry nuclear.

Wall Street raised a further $11 billion additional to Scott's own sum to support Level 3's goal of building the world's first pure IP network. What Level 3 realized, correctly, was that the Internet itself (which is entirely ephemeral and has no tangible "physical being") wasn't the big prize; rather the prize was the protocol (and thus the wires in the ground network) that enabled it to work.

Predictably, imitators followed in the Level 3's wake. A headlong rush into the abyss of creating as much capacity as could be funded (in other words, a lot) was the result. With deregulation occurring simultaneously, the financial markets concluded that these new companies, and perhaps not the former incumbents, would be the key players in the new world of telecoms. They fell over themselves to provide the required support.

The result was a stampede of money searching for an opportunity. Everyone realized the potential of the Internet, the swollen coffers of finance wanted to swell further with a piece of the profit. From private equity investors to venture capital firms, the queue of dollars awaiting a telecoms ride stretched round the metaphorical block many times over.

For all the support they attracted, however, many of these companies were limited in their scope. In nascent form, scale was necessarily limited and had the telecoms collapse occurred more quickly than it did, the crash arguably would have been containable as a sharp blip on the scale rather than the earthquake that it was and still is.

What changed the equation was the decision of long-standing, respected giants from other sectors to move into telecoms and thus prospectively to swell their own balance sheets with a chunk of what resembled the endless pie. Suddenly, serious heavyweights such as the British manufacturing monolith GEC were in on the game (see the case study), in that case selling off traditionally profitable assets and effectively re-inventing itself as the telecoms equipment provider Marconi. A storm in which companies like these collapsed would clearly have different boundaries to the fall of a market in which the players involved were little more than at an embryonic stage, over-capitalized or not.

Marconi, accompanied by others ranging from Scottish Power to Enron, all felt they were equipped to exploit the telecoms opportunity. They had the infrastructure and the general corporate expertise, never mind that they had no experience and apparently even less understanding of the new market they were entering. This, apparently, didn't matter.

They were, furthermore, joined by another tranche of "new" players with histories and financial might equal to their own which again added risk to an increasingly volatile situation. These newcomers were the former incumbent telcos (BT, AT&T, Deutsche Telekom and their ilk), but post-deregulation and desperate to re-invent themselves as aggressive, innovative, and forward-thinking. The pie, they felt, was their rightful inheritance anyway though now they needed to get the new formula right.

Thus what at one stage had been an excitable market peopled by innovative and well funded newcomers had soon evolved into a volatile mixture of powerful balance sheets, highly competitive CEOs, massive corporate hubris, and out-of-control egos. Were something to go wrong in this environment, any resulting fall was guaranteed to be spectacular.

GRAND VISIONS, GRAND FAILURES

Within each segment of the newly constituted telecoms market lay unique and highly specific problems. For the former incumbents bent on maintaining their dominant positions, the legacy of the years of monopoly was problematic. New chief executives might espouse grand visions, but middle management, static and short-sighted, could rarely carry them out and thus held their companies back. To make expensive investments was to be seen to play at the top table in the new world, but the logic and consistency behind many of the acquisitions made was missing. The former incumbents often "acted big" but appeared to have little idea what to do thereafter. Thus, grandiose schemes like Concert, the alliance between former giants BT and AT&T offered much sound and fury but signified almost less than nothing. An apocryphal tale now told is that only in 1998 did AT&T even fully realize the Internet was actually significant. Up to then, it had thought it a craze irrelevant to anyone but amateurs and children. The culture of these companies was conducive neither to rapid progress nor fundamental change.

But all the players in the new telecoms market shared one thing in common. That was a belief that the money tap was turned firmly and permanently to the "on" position. If they wished to make an investment, the funding would be there and the revenue would follow in turn. Quite why they should have assumed this is hard to fathom (though the world of finance, for a long time, gave them every indication that they were right in their assumption), given that the size of the telecoms market was always finite, that household spending on telecoms services is reasonably fixed and is unlikely to vary for any reason in the future, and also that the number of companies seeking to serve and exploit the market was growing by the day.

At some point, increasing market share would no longer be possible. There would simply not be any more money to be made. With this fact allied to the bandwidth glut, added to the investments in futuristic services and the licenses required to offer them (none of which were returning any income on the expense incurred) it was quite obvious that the house of cards was rapidly going to come crashing down.

CASE STUDY

Global Crossing

Global Crossing was founded in 1997 by Gary Winnick, a former junk-bond salesman and associate of fabled (and jailed, albeit since reformed) Wall Street trader Michael Milken. Winnick had seen an opportunity, and that was AT&T's need for an undersea cable that would link Europe and the United States. Within a year, he'd grasped the nettle and the resultant company was selling space on its high-speed voice and data link, and simultaneously raising billions of dollars to create a global fibre optic network in the process.

Winnick and his early investors made fortunes, literally overnight. Via Global Crossing, his own worth was estimated at around $6 billion and he was known as the richest man in Los Angeles for a time in the late 1990s.

Yet by late January 2002, sinking under over $12 billion of debt, Global Crossing had become the largest (at the time) telecoms company ever to file for bankruptcy protection in the United States.

In its heyday (which, frankly, didn't last very long), Global Crossing had been valued at $55 billion, more than General Motors at the time. It is unlikely, after bankruptcy, that its lenders will emerge with more than a tiny fraction of their original investments, and some will emerge empty-handed altogether. Notwithstanding which, the company still insists that Winnick's original strategy of laying cable and selling capacity to telecoms operators and Internet service providers around the globe was valid. WorldCom, at least, had some history. Global Crossing went from nothing to a valuation of $55 billion dollars, to a $12 billion debt crater in the space of less than five years. The story of Global Crossing's implosion is to a great extent the tale of Winnick and his board. It is the story of an egotist who appears to have more or less raped both the market and his employees, whilst walking away with a large share of the profit.

Global Crossing spent around $15 billion dollars during its existence, building the world's most up-to-date fiber network, ultimately spanning four continents, 27 countries and claiming more than 100,000 customers. It collapsed largely for reasons seen in the previous chapter, though company spokesmen have preferred to blame, amongst other things, the recession and the downfall of other upstart telecoms firms for souring the banking environment needed to keep it afloat. The last statement in particular seems rich considering the source.

Winnick himself had always been something of a larger than life figure. A close aide of Milken (*sic*), he left that business relationship before things turned sour for the latter. In 1998, with Global Crossing well on its way, he paid more than $60 million for a single family home (in Los Angeles), believed to be the highest price ever paid in the United States. The home, sadly, needed work so Winnick poured another $30 million into renovations. Such was the inflated style (or lack of it) mirrored by his company.

In an interview with *Business Week* magazine in 2000, Winnick announced that "money's no fun unless you spread it around". His behaviour, for all the world, appeared to be reminiscent of a B-movie version of Gordon Gekko, albeit more idiot than idiot savant as it turned out. Winnick and Global Crossing may have been good at getting their hands on money, but they weren't very good at running a telecoms business.

Global Crossing went public in August 1998 and shares closed at a split-adjusted $9.30 at the end of the first day of trading. Within little more than half a year, that price had risen to $64. Then and over the ensuing years, Winnick personally cashed in more than $600 million of stock. Even when the bankruptcy filing came and GX shares were selling for as little as thirty cents each, Winnick still held around $10 million in the company.

When things got bad for Global Crossing and Winnick, they quickly got worse. A number of investors launched lawsuits in the wake of the bankruptcy filing, alleging that the company and its underwriters had illegally inflated the price of the stock. In its last official reporting quarter, Global Crossing had lost over $3 billion on revenues of just $286 million. It had nowhere near the customers it needed to generate the revenue necessary to support its massive debt pile. The company, in short was a catastrophe.

But there was more to this story than simply incompetence or mismanagement. Global Crossing had been, during its history, knee deep in the business of attempting to buy political influence. Whilst Enron had spent years fine-tuning its own network of lobbyists, Global Crossing had become an instant powerhouse in the business of securing its own way as it sought the help from Washington it needed to expand its international network.

In the 2000 US election, Global Crossing contributed $2.9 million to various candidates and political parties, more than either established telecoms giants WorldCom or Bell South and more even than Enron itself. They gave to democrats and republicans alike; amongst others $31,000 to Republican Senator John McCain who subsequently asked the FCC to encourage the development of undersea telecom cables.

During the summer of 1990, Global Crossing is reported to have spent a quarter of a million dollars at each political party's convention, holding lavish shindigs and providing all the communications services necessary for the conferences. In this way, the company and Winnick personally collected powerful friends and sought to curry favour among the elite. George Bush senior made a speech on behalf of the company in Tokyo and collected $80,000 in stock by way of payment. Some of those shares he sold a year later when the holding was worth millions.

The most staggering feature of these apparent attempts to play among the corporate big boys now appears to be that neither Winnick nor Global Crossing were any better at winning influence than they were at running their telephone company. About all either appear to have been good at was getting and spending money, generally in the most ostentatious way possible.

And it seems to have been, to some extent, all a matter of ego. Where Enron attempted to have doors opened through effective and timely lobbying, Global Crossing's assault on Washington was neither necessary nor always succesful. To be sure, they had small victories but the company's regulatory and legislative requirements were trivial in comparison to the largesse it displayed. Global Crossing essentially used a nuclear device where a mousetrap would have done the job (and spent accordingly). Winnick emerges looking not so much an incompetent as a (very wealthy) egotist of the highest rank. Of such stuff are many American corporate heroes apparently made.

When Global Crossing filed for bankruptcy, it emerged that Winnick had cashed in shares worth $734 million since the company went public in 1998 in spite of the fact that it had never once made a profit. It should be pointed out that doing so was entirely legal, though that will do little to salve the wounds of the company's investors, including its employees. Global Crossing pension savings, for instance, were invested in the company's own stock which could not then be sold for a five year period. Whilst those in the boardroom milked what appeared to be initial success, those in the engine room of the company were being literally bilked.

Now, both the FBI and the Securities & Exchange Commission are investigating the fall of Global Crossing. Former employees claim that earnings were inflated by accounting malfeasance. At the heart of the claim lies the mooted pyramid scheme which also emerges in the course of the WorldCom scandal, that these companies effectively had no customers and simply swapped capacity between each other to inflate their balance sheets.

In August 2002, Global Crossing signed an agreement under which Hutchison Telecommunications, a subsidiary of Singapore-based Hutchison Whampoa, would invest $250 million in the company in exchange for a 65 percent majority interest on its emergence from bankruptcy. Global Crossing's creditors support the agreement, yet only months earlier they had rejected an approach from the same source offering $750 million for 79 percent of the company. Owners of common stock will receive no stake in the reorganised company at all.

Later in the same month, the House Committee on Energy and Commerce escalated its investigation into Global Crossing after further allegations of illegal insider trading and suspect acquisitions of other companies came to light.

A month later, emerging reports suggested that the company had entered a series of deals designed solely to prop up its revenue and meet Wall Street expectations. These deals involved the right to use other companies' telecommunications networks.

As we write, it is clear that the Global Crossing story is far from over. On September 30th emails released by a committee in Washington revealed that Gary Winnick was informed as early as June 2001 of his company's impending fall. At the same time, there was documentation produced indicating that former CEO Leo J. Hindery, Jr had urged Winnick to sell off the company's assets. Within a day, the deposed Winnick had generously (*sic*) pledged $25 million of his own money to help employees affected by the collapse of Global Crossing's stock.

Ironically, if there is a winner in this mess (besides the laughably wealthy incompetents who ran the company into the ground), it is the customer. The new Global Crossing will have less debt, lower costs, more money to fund expansion and the assets and footprint of Hutchison behind it. If the new management team can deliver on potential, Global Crossing II might yet become what Global Crossing itself never became. Let's face it, the new management team can't achieve any less.

The last word in the Global Crossing story should, though, as in the last chapter, go the real victims of a truly epic swindle, the former employees of the company itself, one of whom writes:

> We understand the needs and concerns our customers face, and we enable them to spend hard-earned cash on us rather than finding a real, honest company. They know we hold them accountable for nothing and that we will blame our accounting firm when this charade

falls apart. They know we care about no one except ourselves.

But enough lies from us. Here's what some of you, our loyal and faithful friends, even customers and anyone else screwed by our company has to say . . .

CHAPTER 8

The Great Telecoms Swindle

The telecoms market in 2002

Think about this: you have just read a book describing the spectacular rise, followed by the even more spectacular and dramatic fall of a multi-billion dollar industry.

The axis upon which this story tilts has to a great extent been technological progress. The intial rise was fuelled by the onset of competition, subsequent changes in the way we as consumers use telecoms services, and the promise of even more exciting services to come whose launch lies just around a metaphorical corner. The fall was, to a great extent, brought about because of complications and obligations that arose from the conditions above.

Putting that aside for a moment, if one positive word (as opposed to "swindle") can be said to hallmark the world of telecommunications over the past decade it is probably the word "innovation", the source of the progress to which we earlier referred. As the industry never tires of telling you, its future will stretch even the boundaries of our imaginations.

If you now put this book down and wander over to your telephone, it is a near certainty that should you choose to make a call, you will pay a high price to do so over a low-speed network. Cheap, high speed, broadband Internet connections reach the home mainly in the form of newsprint, as indeed do their futuristic mobile counterparts. Somewhere along the line, this fact is one of the many Great Telecom Swindles. When British Telecom was broken apart from the Post Office (to cite but one example), the art of actually delivering the goods was apparently lost.

THE ROLE OF TELECOMS REGULATORS

As we have seen, many factors bear a causal relationship with the telecoms crash. The significance of each, as the industry lurches through the present recession, is a matter for some debate. In the US, the common argument now is that the FCC, the main telecoms regulator, is in large part to blame for the failure of liberalization because in allowing new entrants to enter the market by piggybacking existing operators (such as the broken up Bell companies) infrastructures, investment was discouraged. The competition that resulted was thus to some extent false.

The same problem appears to be very much true in Europe, where regulators have in general taken an insipid and uninspired approach to tackling the entrenched dominance of the former monopolies. In the UK, BT's grip on the telecoms infrastructure has been loosened only at a tortoise-like pace as it has zealously guarded the local loop, though the former monopoly's own inability to function effectively as an independent has nevertheless ensured that the tortoises remain in the race. Perhaps the energy in some cases devoted to postponing the inevitable – no matter how slowly it might come – might better have been devoted to preparing for the future.

The result of deregulation, in so far as the fruits of a grand design have on occasion been decidedly and unnecessarily limited, have been somewhat disappointing though groundbreaking and of undoubted benefit to the consumer nonetheless. We have seen huge sums of money poured into the telecoms market on the strength, amongst other things, of liberalization being introduced. The payback to date has been substandard, to which injury the crash itself has added only insult. Deregulation was founded on a vision, but the vision to bring it to reality has been broadly lacking from the statement of original intent. It is now clear that more investment will be needed to revive and rebuild the telecoms market and one can only wonder whether investors will be queuing up to provide it given their experiences in this apparently open market to date.

THE INTERNET BOOM

What of the Internet boom? Is the great IP network migration and the forthcoming shift in our usage of telecoms services (*sic*) merely a shadow that the telecoms market has now chased over the precipice by building networks for traffic which will never arrive? There is little doubt that the *Field of Dreams* scenario ("build it, and they will come") energized the business community and resulted in much investment in the course of recent years. Yet that investment has spawned a world wrapped in cable for which, at the present time at least, there is little use and for which, furthermore, they may be no use in the foreseeable future at least. A further problem is that whilst the amount of fibre available grew, simultaneous advances in technology have meant that the capacity of fibre itself has increased vastly more quickly, meaning in fact that less fibre would be needed to carry the same volume of traffic as before, and proportionately less fibre will be needed even as traffic increases. Was no one in the telecoms industry talking to anyone else? We the words "due diligence" altogether absence from the industry's decision-making processes?

Furthermore, the fibre that was laid was duplicated as companies sought to compete against each other. Thus, miles of new fibre simply replicated more new fibre that had already been laid in the ground.

The growth of the Internet (mobile and otherwise) and the next generation network has, surely, been exposed as the greatest error of judgement of all. No one can doubt the course and direction of progress, and there is little question that basic assumptions about the future are right. But simply, no one appears to have been prepared to accept that new technologies and new behavioural patterns take years to take root. Did the development of the cable television industry some fifteen years earlier yield no lessons at all? The telecoms world was proclaiming a revolution whilst it was evolution that was taking place. Did no one realize that Darwin had written a book about the onset of the Internet age a hundred and fifty years before? Evolution takes one thing: time.

The combination of deregulation and the next generation world proved to be a volatile mix. The former created a band of pied pipers, competitive carrier newcomers who splashed money on establishing themselves and building their businesses, and thus they sucked into the vortex only-too-eager-for-the-spotlight established giants who effectively bought into their new rivals business plans and felt they had to compete like-for-like. All, ultimately, were to reach the edge of the cliff. Some have crashed over the precipice whilst others teeter on the brink. Very few stand back at a secure distance at the present moment in time.

And thus, *Götterdämmerung*. When the signal event of 3G licenses saw the market hoist by its own petard, the fall was swift and ruthless. The smart move now, for many who bid, is to simply write off the billions spent (wasted) and to wash your hands of the whole mess. The negative impact of 3G may have been directed at the mobile sector, but once the first domino went down the fallout wasn't limited to a single segment. Competitive carriers in the fixed arena fell into financial disarray as the investment community lost faith in telecoms, in turn taking their equipment suppliers with them. The former incumbents and other giants in general have managed to keep their heads just about level with the waterline, though in real terms their falls have been equally spectacular and only governmental lifebelts (in the form of handouts) keep them from the same fate as many of their newer adversaries. The industry lies in near ruin. It is only to a great extent the largesse of governments that continue to stand behind former monopolies such as France Telecom and Deutsche Telekon that has prevented an even greater implosion than that experienced to date. The former owes 60 billion euros, the latter almost 10 billion more.

WHERE DO WE GO FROM HERE?

What happens next? Well, the telecommunications industry and the companies within it are not going to go away. The Swindle will end, and there will be a rebound albeit only in time. For a start, credibility must be restored and, at present, that is in short supply in the telecoms market. Restoring the faith will involve debt reduction, and in all likelihood a swathe of new chief executives being appointed across the industry. The feeling of the financial markets towards the telecoms sector at present makes it likely that this is some way off.

Furthermore, widespread consolidation is almost inevitable. This will happen first in the crowded mobile market where there are, simply, too many players competing, effectively, for too few minutes and thus too little prospective revenue. What will happen in America to WorldCom and its ilk? Will consolidation be the order of the day there, too? Or will one of the spun-off Bell companies such as SBC, Bell South, or Verizon be allowed by the regulators to complete such an acquisition and thus bypass present legislation which prevents them from entering the long distance market. This solution represents a challenge for the regulators to consider. Where, if any, are the safe bets in telecoms today?

In spite of the present situation, though, the telecoms industry mess does yield opportunities and, indeed, offers up myths the deflating of which may provide some sort of silver lining to the present cloud or reasons for optimism about the future. For one, the disastrous glut in bandwidth may have brought the industry to its knees but it may also speed its recovery. Service providers are purchasers of bandwidth, the raw material of telecoms, and the glut is going to mean that as the market starts to rebound the costs of doing business will be low for those who survive.

THE BENEFITS OF BANKRUPTCY

The damage of so many bankruptcies, notwithstanding their headline-making material, is also over-stated in terms of evaluating the market's future or even present state. Bankruptcy . . . so what? Companies file for bankruptcy as a form of administrative protection and they as often as not emerge leaner and stronger for the experience. Through bankruptcy, they lose debt, drop ineffective product lines at little cost, and generally emerge vastly better off. Paradoxically, bankruptcy ends up hurting the competition as much as the troubled company itself, who must soon contend with a revitalized opponent when it emerges from the process. In the 1980s, the airline industry was collectively even more bankrupt than the telecoms industry is today, but that fact seems to have done little longer-term damage. No, bankruptcy isn't good but to state that it's an end to the road is simply not true. The telecoms crisis is a financial one, and it will emerge more or less intact. The options of the bankruptcy courts do much to ensure that it will do so sooner rather than later.

And what of the Great Telecoms Swindle?

The word "swindle", put simply, is somewhat incorrectly taken to implicitly mean criminal intent. But a swindle, though it is hallmarked by the damage it does, may be hallmarked by a fundamental lack of honesty but does not have to involve actually breaking the law. Were that the case, this would be a swindle committed by a very few. It is in fact a "legal" swindle committed by a multitude.

There seems little doubt in light of the guilty pleas already entered by WorldCom executives that laws were broken in the course of the events described in this book, and that the telecoms crash is at least in some part due to corruption, or exacerbated by it. Furthermore, the fact that a number of individuals have enriched themselves enormously whilst leading their companies (and investors) into the abyss is an enormously distasteful fact, though that does necessarily reflect anything illegal. One thing to emerge from the events about which we write, as well as those at Enron, is that there may be a re-defining of what indeed is legal, ethical, or otherwise, as related to such actions in the short- and long-term future.

If it is proven that laws were broken by figures as senior as Bernie Ebbers or Gary Winnick of Global Crossing, this story will become even more spectacular. But if no laws were broken, their behaviour will likely be considered no more dreadful than it already is. The result of their actions is that millions of investors have lost billions of dollars. But we must ask: is incompetence criminal? Unless multiple new cases of fraud come to light, the fact is that a far greater number of investors have lost even greater sums of money in the telecoms crash through companies which have simply failed for reasons entirely unconnected to malfeasance. WorldCom, to date, is the exception and not the rule. The rule is the many competitive carriers who have now altogether disappeared, and the better-established companies who remain alive only in seriously distressed states.

A SWINDLE OF IGNORANCE

In our view, as we have said in the course of this book, the Great Telecoms Swindle is primarily a swindle of ignorance, misjudgement and folly by people who should have known a great deal better. These people are the real swindlers at the heart of the story.

Were it possible to offer one sweeping remedy to turn the market around and leave those primarily to blame for the crash hanging out to dry ours would be this: simply fire every incumbent chief executive officer in the telecoms market.

The quality (to use the broadest word possible) of the people – like Ebbers and Winnick – who populated the boardrooms of the industry in the 1990s (and thus the pied pipers who led the market into the abyss) was appalling. Time and time again they demonstrated their ignorance of technology, of networks, of the services their companies offered, of infrastructure, even of the simple needs of their customers. The glut in bandwidth was matched by a glut in hubris of equal or greater proportion. That the investing public in whatever form should have entrusted its money to men a frightening majority of whom were good for little other than sweet-talking Wall Street bankers represents a swindle of astonishing proportions. That many of these men should have enriched themselves in the process of displaying such manifest incompetence is a scandal which sorely needs addressing. It should also be noted that the "competent executive class" in the telecoms market (and there is one) has been tarred by their brush as well. Good companies now function with depressed market capitalizations often through little fault of their own. Great leaders have diminished reputations because they are in telecoms.

It is abundantly clear that, in the face of years of directionless leadership in which corporations were built on nothing more than hype, a great many companies in the telecoms market are going to have to learn – to some extent from scratch – what their businesses are about. So much changed so quickly that in the late 1990s the telco market re-invented itself without paying due care – almost without paying any care at all – and when the dust finally settles, the successful business model of the future that should have emerged five years ago will belatedly have to be worked out. What that model is remains to be seen, but the ability to provision services, bill, and communicate with customers, to simply offer the market something it wants – requirements historically almost incidental to the telco – are finally going to have to be taken seriously. That the telecoms market has traditionally had little but contempt for its end user customers is thus another part of the Swindle.

STOCK MARKET PRESSURES

The pressures of the stock market have been, and continue to be, a part of the problem. As long as companies are run with the sole goal of inflated short-term share prices in mind, which has been the case for many in telecoms in recent years, then the chances of correct long-term strategic decisions being made are minimized. It is not just the listed companies that find guilt at their door. Investors, too, must better understand the long-term nature of their commitments and understand their relationships with those companies in whom they invest. Yet, with each party egging on the expectations of the other, the relationship between company and investor has come to resemble a vicious circle. As more and more novice investors have been attracted to the equity markets in recent years, it is not accidental that problems have arisen. To some extent investor ignorance has found the counterpart it deserves in the boardroom.

Ego, too, rears its ugly head in this aspect of the Swindle. Popular culture within a corporate context today places an emphasis on success at all costs rather than on long-term development. The contrast between George Simpson and Lord Weinstock that we see in the Marconi story is the epitome of this problem. Our culture no longer values steadiness in either profit or progress . . . it demands spectacular profit and revolutionary advances today. The Great Telecoms Swindle was largely one industry's response to the pressure of these demands. Even at WorldCom, the crimes recorded to date appear to have been motivated as much by fear of the failure to meet market expectations as for the desire to enrich the individuals involved.

3G is, we expect, going to cloud the telecoms picture for some years yet. There is evidence that limited handset offerings may be slowly emerging from the primordial sludge of the handset manufacturers' laboratories but there is little to suggest that the Brave New World has taken root in the public's consciousness and even less to suggest that it will do so anytime soon. As we write, the flavour of the month would appear to be the camera phone, which the telecoms industry seems intent on promoting as a grand step into the future, as if it can afford to deliver another stumble as it has in the past. What price this radically unnecessary and altogether dispensable advance will somehow fail to give a spectacular lift-off to the technology that thus far has achieved little other than helping to bring the market to its knees?

HAS THE TELECOMS INDUSTRY LEARNED ANYTHING?

One wonders if those in the industry have learned anything from their experience with 3G to date? There is a grudging acceptance that the path to it will not be as rapid or straightforward as originally predicted, but you sense that each subsequent marketing campaign holds the consumer in contempt as it ignores an admission of that fact and baits hook after hook in the forlorn hope that it will stumble upon the one on which the mass market will bite. The telecoms market still seems to want it *now*. As long as it avoids public introspection and measured planning and refuses to communicate intelligently with the customer it will give those it needs on its side to speed the recovery little reason for believing that anything has changed. It seems blithely unaware that sometimes the acknowledgement of bad news can be to present good news in itself.

The market also badly needs to put its most public problems behind it. Resolution of the spate of bankruptcies needs in large part to be achieved . . . WorldCom, Global Crossing and others need to transform themselves into either future success stories or into whatever they are to become. Things must be seen to move on from the present trench.

The lumbering former incumbents in Europe desperately need to fulfil even a fraction of their potential. They need strategic leadership from chief executives who are up to the job (as we described earlier) and they need to either resolve their woeful financial situations by reducing debt mountains or, quite frankly, to be allowed to join their competitors in the bankruptcy courts. It is all very well for those companies to be propped up by their governments but the telecoms market, if healthy, is either liberalized or it is not. The situation with regard to France Telecom and Deutsche Telekom is yet another swindle in itself, though one victim here is, ironically, the telecoms market as a whole. As for the European political penchant for interference, the less said the better.

The service provider market in particular, and the telecoms market in general, also needs to realize that, having effectively outsourced its future in the shape of the research and development of the network to the new breed of equipment supplier, it badly needs those companies (Lucent, Nortel, and others amongst them) to survive and flourish. The Lucents of the world may no longer be a part of one company. Instead, they are actually a part of many. They are not independent in every sense of the word. Weak leadership (*sic*) may have resulted in those players presently teetering on the edge of the abyss, but it is very much in the interests of their customers to do what they can to pull them back. In looking introspectively at themselves, the newly competitive telecoms market needs to take a holistic view of where it stands and to realize common interests as well as competitive ones. Unlikely as it sounds, a degree of co-operation or at least understanding of the facts may well be the basis of healthy competition in future. Put simply, the blind must stop, collectively, leading the blind.

CONTINUING CONTEMPT FOR REGULATIONS

Lastly, though we do not think the Swindle is fundamentally a criminal issue, matters of corporate governance (both within and without the telecoms market) have to be addressed if investor confidence is to be restored. This is a broad point, but an important one. The truth is that for investors, there are significant bargains in the telecoms market right now, which none are going to touch with the proverbial barge pole in the present economic climate.

A renowned fund manager is reported to have said that the term "corporate governance" is little more than a euphemism for the stopping of theft. Yet corporations themselves treat any requirement to conform to a standard of integrity with utter contempt. Even in the wake of present day events, the CEO of Sun Microsystems described signing a document verifying the accuracy of his company's accounts as pointless, nothing more than a cost to his shareholders. The CEO of Dell Computers described the same thing as "socialism".

In which case, roll on the red army. Such contempt for regulation amounts to contempt for the shareholder, and the shareholder today is probably intelligent enough to work that out. Whether because of the many or the few, the Great Telecoms Swindle with its endless revisions of forecasts and restatements of earnings has made it clear that investors cannot trust market leaders to police themselves or, indeed, to honestly provide them with the information they need to make decisions about their companies. Dell and its ilk have only themselves to blame.

For the Swindle to end, stupidity, short-sightedness, ignorance, and hype have to stop. The telecoms market must in the broadest sense decide what it is. Is it a liberalized, competitive market moving slowly towards technical evolution which, ultimately, will benefit its cherished customers and thus reward itself? Or is it faux-liberalized, built on the cornerstone of closed-local loops and ineffectual deregulation, encouraging belief in progressive technological myths and treating its primary revenue sources with contempt? It is a swindle that these questions need answering. It is a swindle that they even have to be asked.

Postscript

The WorldCom saga continues to unfold, and its final resolution – Will it emerge from bankruptcy to some degree intact? Will more criminal charges ensue against its officers? –is not likely to be reached before mid-2003, if by then. Thus the full extent of the Swindle remains to be revealed.

In WorldCom's first financial statement after the accounting scandal was exposed, in October, the company announced that it had lost $429 million on revenue of $4.9 billion in July and August, 2002. Casting these numbers into relief, WorldCom's two biggest rivals, AT&T and Sprint, announced profits for the first time in several quarters. As the latter may suggest that, finally, the telecoms market is starting to stabilize (at least in the long-distance sector), the news may not be as bad it seems for WorldCom. On the other hand, the numbers at AT&T and Sprint were driven by cuts in spending rather than increases in earnings. If a step in the right direction has been taken, it's a small one.

WorldCom delineated its own accounting picture in papers filed with the US Bankruptcy Court in New York. There continues to be speculation that the worst damage the scandal will inflict on the company may not become clear for another twelve months. WorldCom's largest customers are generally locked-in to long-term contracts, and it is only as these come up for renewal that it will become clear how much of its client base will be lost.

In the bankruptcy court hearings WorldCom announced that it had built a cash balance of $1 billion in recent months, doing so because it no longer needs to make interest payments on its debt as part of the bankruptcy protection process.

In the wake of what appeared to be this slight stabilizing of the ship, on October 29th the Swindle leapt back into the news when Stiles A. Kellet, he of the free corporate jet rental and Bernie Ebbers' personal loan approval panel, agreed to resign from WorldCom's board and pay a not revealed sum back to the company related to his use of the jet. By this time, Richard Breeden, the court-appointed monitor, had made clear in a memo to the WorldCom board that he believed the jet lease was a reward for approving the loans to Ebbers and he had urged the board to remove Kellett as a result.

Kellett had argued that there was nothing improper about the one-year lease, though when the board nonetheless demanded his resignation he quickly agreed a settlement rather than engage in a fight about whether his board colleagues had the power to fire him. Magnanimously, Kellet released a statement saying he had decided to step down to save the company from added distractions as it progressed through the bankruptcy process: "Not only does this settlement incorporate reasonable terms, it relieves the company of the improvident risk to removing a director illegally, and hopefully impels it to more constructive action to restore its financial health." Upon the axis of such generosity of spirit do

Swindles apparently revolve. Investors, regulators, and WorldCom itself were doubtless collectively bowled over by Stiles' heroic self-sacrifice.

In early November, an examiner in WorldCom's bankruptcy case suggested that so extraordinary were the illegal steps taken to manipulate its balance sheet that the company would likely have to further restate results beyond those figures already disclosed. The examiner, Dick Thornburgh, said: "A picture is clearly emerging of a company that had a number of troubling and serious issues. These issues relate to the culture, internal controls, management, integrity, disclosures and financial statements of the company."

The involvement of Thornburgh, a former US Attorney General, in the bankruptcy proceeding was unusual since examiners rarely play a role in these cases. The most recent example of one being appointed was for Enron's bankruptcy case. Thornburgh was charged by the presiding judge to oversee WorldCom and investigate and report on issues set out by the court. He quickly concluded that: "Our investigation strongly suggests that WorldCom personnel responded to changing business conditions and earnings pressure by taking extraordinary and illegal steps to mask the discrepancy between the financial reality at the company and Wall Street's expectations."

In the ensuing days, Thornburgh released a preliminary report detailing his findings after a review of over a million documents pertaining to WorldCom operations, including the multi-million dollar loans to Ebbers and company's relations with analysts and investment bankers.

Among initial conclusions, Thornburgh underlined the damning cult of personality through which Ebbers had apparently dominated WorldCom, as he put it "exercising substantial influence over the board's decision-making process and actions" and where "critical questioning was discouraged and the board did not appear to evaluate proposed transactions in appropriate depth."

He added that the board's compensation and stock option committee "seems to largely abdicate its responsibilities to Mr Ebbers. It approved compensation packages that appear overly generous and disproportionate." Effectively, Thornburgh concluded that WorldCom was to a considerable degree driven by Ebbers' personal whims and that the focus of the company was on managing stock price rather than having any serious corporate strategy. Ebbers, and to a lesser extent Scott Sullivan, ran WorldCom flying by the seat of their pants or, as Thornburgh put it:

> It appears that any general strategic planning was in fact done principally by Mr Ebbers, and somewhat lesser extent by Mr Sullivan, and that this planning activity was largely informal, lightly documented and to some extent consisted of oral discussions among a small number of executives.

WorldCom board members, many of whom had large personal interests in the company, had rolled over for Ebbers as they had seen their personal wealth grow due to his perceived leadership during the company's boom years.

Thornburgh's report claimed that Ebbers had effectively awarded himself compensation packages worth an average of $25.7 million from 1999 to 2001. Further, more than $408 million in personal loans to Ebbers were approved by the compensation committee, apparently to cover margin calls on his WorldCom stock. Thornburgh calculated Ebbers' personal and business debt as being in excess of $1 billion.

According to Thornburgh's findings, WorldCom board members were, apparently, not told that Ebbers had used $27 million from the various loans for expenses such as building a house, giving $2 million to a family member and lending $1 million to friends. Ebbers also used $22.8 million to fund his own business interests.

Thornburgh's report further disclosed that WorldCom's accountants, Arthur Andersen LLP, had determined as early as 1999, and repeated in both 2000 and 2001, that the company was a "maximum risk" client although little was apparently done to address concerns this raised.

Andersen responded by claiming that it would be near impossible to uncover fraud committed by a company's management and that WorldCom had duped its auditors as effectively as it had misled investors.

In the wake of Thornburgh's report, the Securities and Exchange Commission expanded its fraud case against

WorldCom Inc., stating that the improper bookkeeping stretched back to at least 1999 and the total amount of fraudulent accounting may exceed $9 billion.

The original charges were amended with the consent of WorldCom, with which the SEC remains in settlement talks. WorldCom has admitted that in the course of these talks it has uncovered further questionable accounting, perhaps bringing the total recorded through improper accounting to over $9.5 billion. Reaching settlement is critical for WorldCom, as it would remove a significant legal burden hindering the future of the company. It is believed that talks are nearing conclusion and may be finished by early 2003, but there is now concern that a new SEC chairman (Harvey Pitt, the incumbent, resigned in the days before this book was completed) will want additional time to review any proposed deal in detail. There is some feeling of surprise that the SEC would settle before many of the WorldCom investigations have been completed. The justice department, amongst others, are still in the midst of their own WorldCom related work.

On November 11th, 2002 it was reported that Bernie Ebbers was considering relinquishing some or all of his $1.5 million annual pension to help settle his $408 million personal loan from WorldCom. By this stage, WorldCom's board had started seizing assets Ebbers had pledged as collateral for the loan, fearing that he would declare bankruptcy. It had become clear that Ebbers had insufficient assets to repay more than a fraction (half at most) of the amount he owed.

The following day speculation began that WorldCom, eager to

put the past behind itself, had informally approved computer industry veteran Michael D. Capellas to be its next chief executive. Capellas – whose curriculum vitae includes an appearance on the cover of *Rolling Stone* magazine dressed in Bruce Springsteen style leathers – had just resigned as president of Hewlett-Packard Co and though with little telecommunications experience (*sic*), he apparently won over WorldCom's executive search committee with his record of turning around a major corporation and putting it up for sale.

The expected announcement of Capellas' arrival was confirmed on Friday, November 15th, when he was formally named WorldCom's chairman and chief executive. His proposed remuneration still had to be approved by the US judge presiding over the bankruptcy case, but this is expected to be a formality.

His track record as an industry leader is founded on steering Compaq through its $19 billion merger with Hewlett-Packard in 2001 having previously revitalized the company in preparation to find a buyer. Nevertheless, telecoms experience is absent from his résumé.

Capellas, predictably given the circumstances, has said he expects to turn Worldcom around and commented "In order to do this, we must first regain trust and win respect. Accordingly, together we will rebuild WorldCom into a model of good corporate governance and management integrity." To do so, it is expected that one of his initial steps will be to revamp WorldCom's board of directors, thereby drawing a clear line between past and future.

On Saturday, November 16th, introducing himself to the company's staff for the first time, Capellas proved an inspiration figure. Though offering few details on his plans for WorldCom and warning that cost cuts were still needed, he suggested that further layoffs were possible and that WorldCom might yet change its name. Though the board was likely to revamped as expected, Capellas confirmed his intention to keep the management team of the company in place.

Capella's "inauguration" suggested that the cult of personality is alive and well in both the telecoms industry and American corporate politics. His new employees at WorldCom's suburban Washington DC location, joined by thousands of others around the country, welcomed their leader to, apparently, the beat of rock music piped through speakers and, as Capellas listed his priorities the workers intoned back "Customers. Customers. Customers."

Capellas, it seems hard to believe, even persuaded WorldCom's senior management onstage with him to join a chorus of "If you're happy and you know it, clap your hands."

Indeed.

But at WorldCom and in the telecoms industry in general happiness should be so easy to find. Where you might think that the fundamental prerequisite of the company's recovery process would be to strive for trust, "whiter than white" status, all may not be as it seems. Cappella's laughter-mantras perhaps obscures clouds that, if history teaches us anything, may yet gather on the horizon. The Swindle will surely not be so easily dispatched by nothing more than a gesture and a friendly soundbite.

When Hewlett-Packard and Compaq, the latter lead by Cappellas, sought to force through their proposed merger some eighteen months ago the mooted deal was always a fragile proposition for shareholders. It is entirely likely that Capellas' pledge at the time to stay on as president of the combined company influenced at least enough of them to ensure that the vote on the merger went through as he sought.

Whilst making those representations, it appears that Mr Cappellas was simultaneously quietly amending his Compaq employment contract which gave him the right to walk away should there be a change of control within the following twelve-month period. Surely some mistake here? Cappellas was the man negotiating the change of control! Was the turkey about to vote for Christmas?

And did we say "right to walk away"? Sorry. What we meant was $14 million payoff. Basically, as reward for completing a merger the success of which (in market terms and therefore for shareholders) would remain entirely unproven for some time, Cappellas negotiated for himself a massive payoff and the right to take a new job at the same time he was making assurances to his Compaq shareholders that he would be committed to staying on and ensuring that the merger worked.

What does that sort of moral or ethical track record qualify you for? You guessed it: CEO of WorldCom. If nothing else, Cappellas and WorldCom (historically) may be a match made in heaven. Cappellas has said that he aims to bring stability and integrity to his new employer through his own personal conduct. We suspect the shareholders of Compaq will take that representation with an unhealthy grain of salt.

It doesn't end there. WorldCom, apparently, gave Cappellas a $2 million signing-on bonus and a salary of $3 million with a guarantee that if either party walks away before the contract is completed, Mr Cappellas will be significantly wealthier than he is now.

If nothing else, the judicial system to which WorldCom remains beholden placed something of a fly in the ointment. Judge Jed Rakoff did not take a benevolent view of the package, noting that "a compensation package so potentially problematic raises serious concerns as to whether proposed new management is as committed to reform as the nature of this case requires."

Certainly, and in broad terms, the revelations of corporate mismanagement that have come to light over the past twenty-four months and apparently are still continuing have thrown up nothing if not the issue of what appears to be a serious lack of ethics in the boardroom. At the heart of the implosion of the telecoms market, not to mention the broader equity markets, failing performance has not alone engendered the mistrust that is rife today among investors and other market observers.

Corporate history is littered with failed companies whose managements were not up to the job, but those incompetent leaders did not usually bring entire markets down with them.

It is not, thankfully, littered with crooks. The lack of trust has become at least the equal of the lack of sales in terms of the problems markets (and the telecoms market in particular) face today.

You might think, in light of this fact, that as the commercial world seeks to emerge from its most recent darkest hour that it would place an emphasis on a renewed commitment to ethical standards. But if that would appear logical, don't bet your house that it'll happen. As we've just seen at WorldCom, where you might think that if nowhere else, "by the ethical book" would be the order of the day, it apparently isn't.

Oh well, never mind the lack of moral fibre or the absence of telecoms experience. Meet the new boss...same as the old boss. Swimming in the wake of the Great Telecoms Swindle, should that really come as any surprise? For the present, the telecoms market continues to provide a depressing experience for those directly and indirectly involved in it. One suspects that, even now, many of its leaders choose to live in blissful ignorance of the state they're in.

Index